A LITTLETON LAD...
IN HIS OWN WORDS

Born in the village of Littleton, north of Winchester in Hampshire, Austen Hooker attended Crawley village school and Peter Symonds Grammar School in Winchester. When he left school he joined his father and grandfather on the family nursery where he would spend his entire working life and witness many changes. As a teenager he remembers the war years and the effect it had on the villagers. He has enjoyed various local activities, playing sport, singing in operatic productions together with a spell as a radio and TV gardener.

His greatest loves are his family, the village community and the countryside.

Austen Hooker

A LITTLETON LAD…
IN HIS OWN WORDS

AUSTIN & MACAULEY
PUBLISHERS LTD.

Copyright © Austen Hooker

The right of Austen Hooker to be identified as author of this work has been asserted by him in accordance with section 77 and 78 of the Copyright, Designs and Patents Act 1988.

All rights reserved. No part of this publication may be reproduced, stored in a retrieval system, or transmitted in any form or by any means, electronic, mechanical, photocopying, recording, or otherwise, without the prior permission of the publishers.

Any person who commits any unauthorized act in relation to this publication may be liable to criminal prosecution and civil claims for damages.

While every attempt has been made to portray accurate information throughout this book the author wishes to remind the reader of his current age and apologises for any errors which may have occurred.

A CIP catalogue record for this title is available from the British Library.

ISBN 978 1 84963 161 7

www. austinmacauley. com

First Published (2012)
Austin & Macauley Publishers Ltd.
25 Canada Square
Canary Wharf
London
E14 5LB

Printed & Bound in Great Britain

To My Family

Acknowledgements

The Littleton Local History Group and its members.

The Hampshire Record Office.

The Hampshire Chronicle.

The Friends of King Alfred Buses.

The Winchester Operatic Society.

Sarsen Press for all the help and advice on producing the draft copy.

Fred Montague for his advice and help.

Mrs Sheila Trussler for permission to reproduce David Trussler's panorama of Littleton in the year 2000.

Photographs:

Barbara Elsmore, Brian Gill, Brian Holloway, Bruce Parker, Neil Saint, Bob Sollars, George Walsh, Gerry Way, Diana Wilkins.

When we first moved to Littleton I was very much involved with my own personal life and did not give a lot of thought to the village and the community I lived in. While making our new garden we would visit the local nursery to buy plants and if we were lucky we might exchange a few words with Austen Hooker and as often as not this would involve someone from Littleton's past. One of the first people I was introduced to in this way was Horrie Saint on part of whose land, devastated by the building of our new bungalow, we were now trying to re-establish a garden. Austen told me Horrie trained at Hilliers just like his own father and that he was an expert on fruit trees planting many in our part of the village. He added that Horrie also used to organise the village whist drives which entailed making the tea and being a careful man he would not be overgenerous with the teabags and would subsequently receive a regular gentle ribbing from the card players on the strength of his tea. Back home again I would look at the old fruit trees all around me together with all the glass bottles and jars and old bits of metal that I would dig up from time to time and now I fancied that I had been given a little window into the past by Austen. Now nearly thirty years later and armed with my laptop and scanner and Austen with an old tape recorder he has found at the back of a drawer we are going to make a start at recording his memories and stories. Austen has given me carte blanche to re-write or re-phrase anything he has dictated but as I read through the results of the first tape I realise that nothing needs to be changed at all as this is Austen's story **A LITTLETON LAD** told entirely... *"in his own words"*.

Barbara Elsmore
November 2008

INTRODUCTION

As a boy and young man I spent much of my time on the nursery with Dad and Grandad. They would tell me stories of their past and how they came to Littleton and started the market garden and nursery. At meal times the conversation would often be about cricket and other village activities and how the community spirit had developed.

Life moves on and today's families become more widespread and consequently there is less day-to-day opportunity to tell of family history. I hope David, Andrew, Kate and Samantha will find my memories of past family life interesting and that in years to come they will be able to add theirs to the family story.

Because I have lived in the village of Littleton all my life, several of my friends have been trying to encourage me to write my life story. I think it was my dislike of anything which might keep me indoors and remotely connected with office work which made me delay making the effort to get down to putting pen to paper. Talking is one of the things I'm often reminded of by my friends and family is something that I do a lot of. When Barbara suggested why not record your memories on tape and we will write them up I really didn't have an excuse to delay any longer. For the last 18 months I have recorded a tape about once a month. Barbara's sister-in-law, Pam Elms, has then transformed my ramblings from the tape into print, and then passed them on to Barbara who edited them if necessary. Connie proof read them and together we made any alterations before Barbara collated them with the photos and poems. Without the patience, encouragement and skill of Barbara, Pam and Connie I would not have been able to achieve the project and to them I would like to record my grateful thanks.

Austen Hooker

What strange mysterious links enchain the heart
To regions where the morn of life was spent.
James Graham

Contents

INTRODUCTION   15

TAPE 1   19
The Family

Tape 2   20
Early Memories

Tape 3   26
Pre-school days

Tape 4   34
School Days

Tape 5   49
Growing-up

Tape 6   65
The War Years

Tape 7   85
Working on the Nursery

Tape 8   99
Recreational Interests

Tape 9   110
Winchester Operatic Society

Tape 10   **121**
   Early Married Life

Tape 11   **135**
   Family Life

Tape 12   **147**
   The Growing Nursery

Tape 13   **159**
   From Opera to Television

Tape 14   **172**
   Clubs and Associations

Tape 15   **184**
   The Community

Tape 17   **203**
   Contemplations

TAPE 1
The Family

'The family' in 1952 Anne, Dad, John, Mum, myself and little brother Richard in front with his bat and ball – taken in Horsham where we were playing cricket for Crawley

Principle members of the Hooker and Goater Families

Austen Hooker married:	Connie Smithers
Paternal Grandparents:	Fred Hooker married Jane Newell
Maternal Grandparents:	Lewis Goater married Emeline Kate Smith
Father:	Bill Hooker married Norah Goater
Sister:	Anne
Brothers:	John and Richard
Sons:	David married Jackie Dudman
	Andrew married Nikki Bourne
Granddaughters:	Kate and Samantha

Tape 2
Early Memories

Being lifted on to the potting shed bench, where Dad was mixing his potting compost, is among my earliest memories. Like most nurserymen, he had his own recipe. I can remember, I quite liked the smell of the bonemeal which he mixed in, but I was not so fond of the smell of the fishmeal. He would first have to riddle the soil, which came from a large heap of stacked turf which was collected some year or two before. Peat was not used in those days, so he would have had to collect leaf mould. Silver sand was also mixed in. The combination of these ingredients mixed together would be made up into his potting compost. He might have varied it slightly for different plants. This was before the days of John Innes compost.

As I grew up, Dad and Grandad would recall stories to my brother, John, and myself. Among these, was of how they first came to Littleton to start a market garden and nursery. Grandad was brought up in Horndean. He lost his father at a young age and his mother married again. There was a large family, of which he was the eldest. He left school at the age of 12 and started work on a local farm near Rowlands Castle. In those days the only way a boy could get off the land was to join the army, which Grandad did. He joined the Rifle Brigade, which brought him to Winchester for the first time. A large part of his army life as a regular soldier was spent in India, where most of his time was taken up looking after the General's polo ponies.

When he left the army he married Granny and lived at number 36 Tower Street in Winchester, where his three children were born. In the late 1890s he took over a small general shop in Western Road, Winchester. Shortly after that the Boer War broke out and because he was a reservist he went back into the Army and was sent to South Africa. This left Granny looking after three small children as well as looking after the shop. However, this did not last too long as Grandad developed rheumatics in South Africa and was invalided out of the army. Granny was told she would have to look after him for the rest of his life, but Grandad had other ideas. By 1907 he had made an almost complete recovery and had built up his shop in Western Road.

Nearby in the village of Littleton a large amount of land was auctioned for development. Grandad decided to buy three plots for £63. This was about one acre. This he cultivated to grow produce for his shop. In 1908 he had the chance to buy another two and a half acres of land joining his first plot, that giving him a total of three and a half acres. This he turned into a market garden and smallholding, with a small paddock on which he kept chickens, ducks, turkeys and pigs.

Many of the plots were bought up and turned into smallholdings and market gardens. Some were bought by Winchester people just to turn into gardens and somewhere to go for the weekend. They would camp on the plot overnight in the summer months. Some of the plots were gradually built on. Grandad often said that when he first came to Littleton there was nothing from Harestock to the Running Horse.

One of the very first buildings to go up in Littleton was Grandad's stable. This was quite a grand building for its time. It was built of wood, with a straw and matchboard lining for insulation. It consisted of a garage with a pony van at one end, a stable in the middle and a cookhouse with a copper boiler at the other. Over the top was a loft to keep the hay, straw and many other things. This building was still there 90 years later, when the business closed. When he had got all this under way, he found he was producing more than he could sell in his shop in Winchester, so he bought a pony and cart and started a door-to-door round in Winchester.

Another of my early memories was going on the round with Grandad. We would run ahead and knock on the doors for him. His son, my father Bill, often recalled how as a schoolboy he would walk out from Winchester, about a mile and a half, to help his father on the market garden. In the evening they would have to walk back to Winchester to home and the shop in Western Road. There was no such thing as public transport. They would sometimes cycle, but the roads were so bad, no tarmac, they spent a lot of their time mending punctures. On warm summer nights they might sleep over in a shed.

On 1st February 1910 Dad started work for Hilliers in the West Hill Nursery on the Romsey Road opposite the hospital, the site of their present garden centre. In the summer it was very long hours, 6.00 in the morning until 6.00 at night, half day Saturday, finish at 4.00 p.m. His wages were four shillings a week. By the time he got home in the evening and had his meal he was too tired to go out with his friends. He always said he started at the bottom of the nursery business, cleaning out the ash from the stoke hole which was a very dirty job, but he soon progressed to more responsible jobs of potting, propagating and pruning and many other things concerned with the growing of plants, the love of which remained with him all his life.

It was a good grounding, and in 1912 he left and joined his father and started a nursery with a market garden. The first thing they did was to build a greenhouse, which according to Dad's records produced a wonderful crop of tomatoes.

Unfortunately two years later the First World War broke out and Dad left to join the army. He spent the first two and a half years of his life in the army in India, before going on to Palestine, where he was wounded, and then on to France and finally the end of the war in Germany, having been wounded twice. He kept a wonderful diary most of the time.

In 1916 Grandad was left £500 by an uncle and with this he built his house and moved to Littleton to live, having given up the shop in Western Road. He called the house 'Quetta' because that's where Dad and Uncle Fred were stationed in India when the house was built.

At this time other parcels of land in Littleton were being built on including 'Bercote'. Bert Portsmouth, a Winchester baker, placed an ex-railway carriage on his plot which became known as 'Bert's Cott'. The house he built there later was called Bercote giving its name to Bercote Close.

Next door to Bercote was 'Macrocarpa' lived in by Mr and Mrs Horrie Saint and their son Reg. Like Dad, Horrie had also trained at Hillers and was an expert on fruit trees. He planted fruit trees throughout his large plot and over into South Drive, many of which remain dotted around various gardens to this day.

During the war years Grandad kept the whole lot going, with just the help of Granny and his daughter, aunt Flo. This is a man who had been invalided out of the army. When Dad left for the war he was living in Winchester, but in January 1919 he came back to live in Littleton. The first thing they did on the nursery was to build another greenhouse. This, like the first one, was 50'x12' and this one was divided in the middle so that one half could be kept at a different temperature to the other for cucumbers at one end and tomatoes at the other. Some of the old records Dad kept are very interesting. He wrote "*After four and a half years in the army, I found life at home very pleasant, but quite missed the company of many people close at hand. However, I soon started work on the home estate and the time passed very quickly. We had another greenhouse built which we soon filled with cucumbers, mint and various plants. My father now had pigs, a flock of chickens, some ducks, turkeys plus the pony and cart to look after. Any spare time he spent growing vegetables. My mother and sister helped with the flowers and fruit picking. It was a real family business. During the winter time we killed a pig about every fortnight and sold it in the village and around the town. We made sausages, brawn etc. We lived like fighting cocks. We had our own vegetables and apples so were very much self-contained*". The total income for 1920 was £569.19s.8p. This rose to £624.6s.9p in 1921. This is surprising as he wrote in his notes *"There has been only one good night's rain from April until the end of September. Most of the crops were very poor, but the tomatoes and cucumbers have been excellent. "* The turkeys did well, so they must have liked the fine weather.

In the early 1920s Dad played a few games of cricket mid-week for Sparsholt. He also went to the local dances and whist drives at Littleton, Crawley and Sparsholt, and I think this is where he met Mum. Mum lived with her aunts at the village post office and bakery in Sparsholt. She was born and brought up in Southampton, but her mother died when she was 13, so she came to live and work with her aunts Nell and Alice, who ran the bakery and post office together with their brothers. She helped deliver the bread around the villages of Sparsholt, Littleton and Crawley. Mum and Dad were married on 13th April 1925 and they had a bungalow built at the same time on the nursery by Mr Fairhead, a builder who lived in the village, at a cost of £500. My brother John was born on 4th March 1926 and I arrived two years later on 20th April 1928.

Most of the instances I have recorded so far are those that have been told to me many times by my parents and grandparents, especially Grandad. He was a great talker. I have often been told that I am like him.

We'll talk of sunshine and of song,
And summer days when we were young;
Sweet childish days, that were so long
As twenty days are now.
William Wordsworth

This is the old shop in Western road. Connie & myself and the Bosley family at the opening of a replica of the shop now in the city museum

Grandad outside the new stable and cookhouse in 1911

Many years later in 1983 Richard, John and myself outside the stable and cookhouse

Grandad on his way home to tea with his jacket over his shoulder taken in the same spot some 20 years later than the photograph below

Grandad working on his market garden in 1911 being watched over by his dog Rover. Mr Simpson who lived at 'Withens' across the road is picking peas

This is 'Macrocarpa' built by Horrie Saint. It is typical of the homes that were first built on many of the plots in Littleton

'Quetta' bungalow which Mum and Dad had built on the nursery in 1925 when they were first married and in which I was born in 1928 and lived most of my life

Tape 3
Pre-school days

We would spend a lot of our time, before we started school, helping Dad and Grandad on the nursery. We also ventured sometimes on to the recreation ground, which was next door. This had been purchased by the Parish from Mr. Bostock of Lainston House and cricket was first played there in 1921. The rec., as it was known, was not mown right over like it is today. The only part mown was the cricket pitch, or cricket field, in the middle. The top and the bottom of the field were allowed to grow, which was wonderful for us kids to make tracks to crawl through.

In the late summer it was always a special occasion when it was cut for hay. Charlie Cox, a carter from Littleton Stud, arrived with a grass mower pulled by two large horses. I remember I followed him round and round the field all the evening. I still remember the smell of the newly mown grass, especially the wild mint which grew at the top of the recreation ground. When the grass had been cut us kids used to make camps, cars or anything else that our imagination could think of. We were very disappointed when the hay was taken away. Grandad would have had some of it for his pony.

I had a friend who I used to play with called Bob, who lived in Hollands Close. He also had a twin sister Ruby. One day I remember we climbed a tree in the recreation ground. I went up first, Bob followed. When we decided the time had come to get down, he got stuck halfway and he had to get his sister to run home and get his Mum to help him down. He told me many years later that his Dad and older brother never let him forget it.

When I was about two or three I had to go into hospital for three days to have my tonsils out. Apparently I cried the whole time, but Mum was not allowed to see me because they said it might upset me! I don't remember anything about it or what happened, all I can remember now is the smell of the ether.

I was always very fond of my Grandad and spent a lot of time with him in the market garden. From a very early age we were always encouraged to help. It might be feeding the animals or planting and picking up the potatoes. As we lived close by we were often invited to tea by Granny and Grandad. All the meals were eaten in the kitchen. Granny cooked on a black kitchen range, or perhaps in the summer on an oil stove. There was no gas or electricity, just an oil lamp for light and a candle to go to bed. Before we had our tea we had to wash our hands. This entailed pulling a chair up to the kitchen sink so that we could reach the tap. I remember the soap; this was always a purple colour and seemed rather gritty. We then had to stand on another chair to view the mirror to brush our hair. Our quiff, as Grandad always called it. When we had done this we were allowed to sit at the table. Tea was usually bread and butter and jam or perhaps Shippams meat paste to start with. Sometimes it could be some of Grandad's lovely pink celery, or dip-in, as he liked to call it, because you would dip the celery in the salt before eating it. This was followed by Granny's fruit cake washed down with some very strong tea.

With my grandparents everything had to be on time. They lived by the clock. They also lived well. Breakfast at half past seven with bacon, eggs and perhaps some cold bacon or a kipper, followed by bread and butter and marmalade. Dinner was half past twelve and was usually hot, except on Monday, wash day, when it was cold meat from the Sunday roast, with bubble and squeak. This was always followed by a pudding. Granny made a wonderful spiced bread pudding. Tea was at half past four and supper at nine which was also quite a meal. It could be soup; or something left from dinner and heated up. They lived well, with most of the food produced by themselves. No wonder Dad wrote in his diary that they lived like fighting cocks.

Grandad would take us sometimes in the pony and cart on his rounds to Winchester. Brother John was allowed to occasionally drive the pony, Joe, from door to door, although Joe would know most of the customers, especially the ones where he got a sugar knob, John often said he must have been one of the last people to drive a horse and cart through the Winchester Westgate. We always finished up at the shop in Parchment Street, usually about mid-day, whilst Grandad would unload the vegetables from the nursery and load up the empty boxes and baskets. Our treat then was to be taken over the road to Portsmouth Bakery, where they had a small café and where we were treated to a drink and a bun. We were usually served by Miss Portsmouth who, in later years when her parents retired, came over the road and took up the running of our shop. When Joe needed new shoes we would have to stop on the way home at the blacksmiths in Stockbridge Road, which was between City Road and the bridge. I can still remember the smell of the forge and the burnt hoof.

Sometimes, before we came home, we would have to go out to Winnall gasworks, which seemed quite a long way, to collect a load of coke to bring back with us for Dad's greenhouse boilers. This was a heavy load for poor old Joe, the pony, and Grandad and us boys would have to walk up all the hills on the way home.

One of the occasions in Winchester in those days would have been the autumn chrysanthemum show, which was run by the Winchester Horticultural Society. It would be held in the Guildhall and would have been over two days, with quite a large number of people attending. There were long tables down the middle of the hall, one with chrysanths of all colours, shapes and sizes. The ones I remember most were the great big incurves as big as a baby's head. Another table would be of vegetables and another of fruit and all along one side under the balcony would have been wonderful collections of vegetables. In front of the stage would be a trade stand display of shrubs and flowers by Hilliers. On the stage was another trade exhibit, which could have been by Jeffreys, who had a nursery in St. Peter Street. Dad and Grandad would have their stand and exhibit at the other end of the hall under the balcony. In the banqueting hall there would have been groups of chrysanths in pots entered by the professional gardeners from some of the large gardens and estates in the area. This would also include the Headmaster of Winchester College's gardener. On the last evening Mum would take us to help clear up the stand. I remember how I enjoyed running up and down the stairs, stairs I would get to know some years later.

Because Dad mixed silver sand into his compost, he always kept it in a pit just outside the potting shed door, so we boys always had a small pit in which to play. If it was a wet day Grandad would sometimes spend time in the woodshed cutting up logs for the fire. He would sit us on the log on the sawing horse while he was sawing away with a very old rusty cross cut saw. As we got older he would let us help by pulling the opposite end of the saw. He would tell us off if we pushed instead of pulled, as this jammed the saw.

When I was about four, he took me in the pony and cart to Crawley, where he planted some shrubs in front of the church, I think they are still there, and some trees by the War Memorial. As we came back by the school the Headteacher, Mrs. Fish, came out to talk to Grandad. She was one of his customers in Winchester. In conversation she asked him when I was going to start school, but I don't think I was too happy about that.

Christmas was nearly always spent at Sparsholt at the bakery and shop with all the aunts. This was always a very happy time. On Christmas Eve Dad would have to work late at the shop in Winchester making sure all the late deliveries had been done. Mum, John and myself would have to go on to Sparsholt. We were transported by Mr. Hillary, who was the local coalman, but he also ran a small taxi service. I can remember looking up into the starlit sky and seeing shooting stars, and imagining it was Father Christmas flying across the sky. We would be greeted by the aunts, all bent on spoiling us. Dad would arrive later, sometimes after we had gone to bed. It was a wonderful place to spend Christmas, with the shop still decorated for Christmas and the bakehouse with all its enticing baking smells. A lovely feature of the old house was its chimney, which had a bacon loft, where at one time bacon had been smoked. If you looked up you could see the sky and also the iron rungs which were used to climb up to the bacon loft. We were told Father Christmas used these when he came. On Christmas morning there was always some soot in the grate at the bottom. One of the bedrooms of the old house was turned into a bathroom. The water was supplied by a hand pump from a copper below. The room also had a single bed in which John and myself slept. Like most children, we were always awake early on Christmas morning to open our presents. Mum told us that in her young days on Christmas morning folk from the village would bring their turkeys, chickens etc. to be cooked in the bakehouse oven. The ones they had at home were not large enough to take the Christmas birds. Christmas dinner was always a large meal with all the trimmings. The pudding was always set alight and we couldn't understand why it didn't burn. The meal was always followed by a piece of stem ginger out of a stone jar, a tradition we still keep today. The afternoon would have been spent playing with our new toys, or, if fine, going for a short walk with some of the younger aunts. When the adults had their glass of wine, we had a kind of grape juice, which Aunt Nell called "boys' wine". Christmas tea always comprised wonderful crisp celery out of the garden and, of course, Christmas cake made in the bakery and crackers out of the shop.

On Christmas evening we would go down the road to Redthorn, where Uncle Sid lived. Here we would meet up with a lot more uncles, aunts and cousins. As the shop was the post office it was also the manual telephone exchange which covered Littleton, Crawley and Sparsholt, so there always had to be someone there to man it. This meant one of the aunts had to stay behind. Dad said he couldn't leave an aunt there on her own, so he would stay with her. When everyone had got their drinks and inspected the Christmas tree, Father Christmas would arrive. We didn't know until a few years later that this was Dad.

On Boxing Day we would keep a look out for the Hunt, but I can't say that I ever saw it, and in the afternoon we would all go out for a walk with some of the younger relations. In the evening we would have to come home sat in the back of one of the little Dennis buses belonging to the King Alfred Bus Company. The village WI Christmas tea party was an occasion we looked forward to. Long tables were decked out down the centre of the hall. There would be sandwiches, cakes and, of course, jelly. After tea the tables would be cleared away to make way for a conjuror, or sometimes a Punch and Judy. This would be followed by party games, usually pass the parcel, with everyone passing on as quick as they could so that they didn't have to perform a forfeit. The evening finished with some dancing. This was especially for the older children, perhaps encouraging them to come to the village dances.

All this took place in the village Memorial Hall, a place where I would spend some of the happiest times of my life. Grandad and Dad were always proud of the Village Hall and told us many stories of how it came to be built. One they loved to tell was about a meeting which was held in an ex-army hut situated on the old recreation ground on Flowerdown. It was shortly after the end of the First World War and they were there to decide on a memorial for those who had been killed from the village. They decided that they just didn't want a stone, but something which would be useful for future generations. A village hall was suggested. Most of the village were there and consisted of people from all ranks of life. The question now was – how were they to raise the money? Apparently at this point Grandad got up from his seat, turned to the assembly and said "*how many times over the last four years have I heard people say what would I give to wake up tomorrow to find the war is over. Well, the war is over and now is your time to give*. "An old sailor sauntered up to the platform and, placing some money on the table, said to the chairman, "*Here is a starter for you*". It really was, for within a few minutes over £200 was given. After all, they couldn't be shown up by a poor old sailor. Grandad never did let on as to whether he had set it up. By 1925 the £725 was raised and the hall built.

It must have been one of the first tragedies of my life when my brother John and myself were looking over the sty at the pigs. As it happened I had my teddy bear with me. John took it from me to show it to the pigs and promptly dropped it. Before we could get Grandad to get it back the pigs had eaten it. I didn't like the pigs for a long time after that.

Thou happy day of sound and mirth
That long with childish memory stays,
How blest around the cottage hearth
I met thee in my boyish days.
John Clare

Littleton's first cricket team about 1920 they played on Harestock Corner with Kennel Lane. Dad is seated in the middle without cap and uncle Fred is behind him

I was about three years old and sitting on the lawn outside the bungalow around tonsil removal time

John and myself sat on Grandad's cart pulled by Joe the pony

The main road through the village as I remember it in the 1930s on the right is the pond covered in bushes and on the left is the beech tree and the house 'Hillsbrough' both still there

Uncle Sid and great grandfather Goater stand very proudly in front of the new bakers' van in the 1920s

Old hall built in the 1920s. Some of the happiest times of my life were spent in it

Tape 4
School Days

In April 1933 I started my schooldays at the little village school in Crawley. To go to school we had to wait for the bus at the end of Fairclose Drive. The bus was one of the old King Alfred Albions. I still remember the number now. Number OU 1704.

The infant teacher, Miss Sillence, whose class I was to be in, would be waiting there too. She lodged during the week at number 8 Hollands Close. I think her family were farmers who lived in Twyford. One morning my cousin Bill ran across the road and was knocked over by Miss Morgan, who was riding her bike down the road on her way to work. Fortunately neither was hurt. Miss Morgan went on to live in the village until she was well over 100. On the bus would be the other two teachers, Mrs. Beale, a widow, and Mrs. Fish, the Head. The school bus would have travelled up the Andover Road from Winchester, picking up the first children at Harestock Corner. They would then have gone on towards Andover and turned up through Flowerdown to the village. On through the village to Crawley, picking up children on the way. By the time it reached the school it could have been quite full. I sometimes had to sit on my brother's knee.

The school consisted of three classrooms, a small hall, a teachers' room and two cloakrooms. The playground was small and was of rough gravel, not very suitable to run on and produced many grazed knees, mine included. We still had slates to write on for the first year or two. If somebody had a loose tooth, they didn't dare start to wriggle it about, because if you did Miss Sillence would produce a blackboard duster and pull it out. We had to take our own mid-day meal, which usually consisted of sandwiches, sometimes a pie, a piece of cake and fruit, orange, apple, pear etching remember making the other children laugh when I squeezed my over-ripe banana. I cannot say that I liked school all that much. I always wanted to be out in the fresh air, so I was very pleased when later on I got the job of looking after the school garden, which ran along the side of the school. This I had to water in the summer months. Unfortunately I had to spend most of my lunch break trying to improve my spelling. I don't think it did me much good. The problem was that spelling held me back in other subjects, although I did not have the problem with reading and sums.

The one thing I did enjoy at Crawley School was the musical plays which were performed once a year in the village hall. My last two years there I was given a leading part. The first year we were all made up like dolls. I was a coloured doll and had to have my face blacked, which I much enjoyed. I didn't want to wash it off afterwards. The second year most of the children played months of the year and I was the clerk of the weather trying to make them behave, the month of March causing the most trouble! I carried a cut-out cardboard barometer.

One of the things that did upset me rather were the toilets. They were back in the dark ages, consisting of a bucket and soil. I had been used to the flush toilet at home and this came to me as a bit of a shock. This had also been of some concern to the Parish Council and an unfortunately worded minute of the Parish Council dated 9th April 1934 reads *"The sanitary arrangements at Crawley School were very poor. For some time it was impossible to get the buckets emptied. This has now been rectified and the matter was allowed to lie on the table."*

We didn't have any real organised sport at school, only drill, as it was called. A sort of PT with competitions at which we wore different coloured braids. If you misbehaved you were given the cane on your hands, not very nice. Brother John was much quieter and better behaved than me, he only got the cane once in all the time he was at Crawley, and that was for throwing a snowball at a boy. Unfortunately he missed the boy and hit Mrs. Fish just as she was coming round the corner. John's usual bad luck. I know I got the cane several times, once for making out I was conducting the class when Mrs Fish was out of the room, but she still gave me the best part in the school play.

My favourite time was Friday afternoons, because it was near the end of the week and we had a story read to us. At 3.30 we queued up in the playground in the same order as we got on the bus in the morning. The further you had to go the further you went up the bus. The bus had a kind of well at the back which formed a platform for people to get on and off. You then went up a step into the main body of the bus. The well had seats around it on two sides which went right up to the door. It was all boys who sat there and the best seat was considered to be next to the door, so as you got older in the school so you would work your way round until you had the prize seat next to the door. The bus, when full of children, had a great job to struggle up the steep hill from Crawley Pond. Once the bus dropped us off I would tear home, change into my old clothes and rush out into the rec. where we would meet up with our friends and get stuck into playing whatever game was in season.

Although we didn't have any sport at school, the village always seemed to turn out plenty of sportsmen and sportswomen, mainly because we were always playing some sort of sport on the recreation ground, which had been bought for the Parish from Mr. Bostock. Apparently it came about when Grandad and his friend Ike Hillier, who were very keen on cricket, were looking for a field to play in. The site which they thought would be right was the six acre field next to grandfather's nursery and market garden. Dad says in his diary *"My father and Ike Hillier walked over to Lainston House and had a chat with Mr. Bostock, who owned the field. He was also a keen cricketer and agreed to sell them the field for sport."* I've often imagined Grandad going up to the door of the big house and saying *"Please can we buy your field?"* The money was raised by the parishioners and the Parish Council and cricket was first played in 1921 and tennis followed shortly after.

Another reason to hurry home from school would have been that Grandad had a sitting of eggs ready to hatch under the broody hen. The hen would have been sitting on about 13 eggs for three weeks and would have been kept in a large box separate from the other hens and allowed out to feed once a day. Grandad would lift the hen off to see whether all the eggs had hatched. Some could have been infertile. The average would have been about ten chicks. These we would lift out and put into a wooden gallon measure. We would then set off with these to put them in a chicken coop in the paddock, Grandad carrying the hen, who would be rather disturbed and agitated while we carried the chicks. Within a few days they would be running around behind the old hen. Sometimes a sitting of ducks eggs would be put under the hen. These took an extra week to hatch. When the ducklings took to the water, the hen would get very agitated, thinking they were going to drown.

My days at Crawley School came to an end in April 1939 having been there for six years, two in each class. Unlike John, I didn't pass the scholarship for Peter Symonds and had to go to the senior school at Stanmore, like several of the other boys in the village. The girls went to St, Mary's, which was near the Abbey Gardens behind the Guildhall in Winchester. Mum arranged for me to go and have my mid-day meals with her cousin, Win, who lived in Stanmore. John had done this when he was in Stanmore for one term before he went on to Peter Symonds. When the day came for me to start at Stanmore I went off with several who had been at Crawley and my new friend Alan Gill, who had just come to live with his two young brothers, Eddie and Brian, in the bungalow next to my grandparents. He, like John, had passed the scholarship, but had to spend one term at Stanmore before starting at Peter Symonds in September.

Stanmore School was very modern for its time and was built in a U-shape to take the children from the large Stanmore Estate which was developed between the wars. The classrooms had glass on two sides, which opened up in the summer, the whole lot connected by an outside corridor, with a large hall connecting the two sides forming the bottom of the U. When we arrived at the school we were ushered to the Head's study. He said they could not take us in as the school was already full. We were then bundled off to St. Thomas' School, which was at the top of Winchester near the railway line. We had to find our own way without any supervision.

St. Thomas' was very different to Stanmore. This was the same old school Dad had been to 30 years before. Here, we were put into two classes, one for the brightest and the other for the rest. I was put with the rest. Here again I think my spelling must have let me down, but as it turned out at the end of the term it was the only time I came out top of the class in all my schooldays, not that this said much about my scholastic abilities. When I got home after our first day at senior school and told mum what had happened, she was rather cross, and that's putting it mildly. After all the arrangements she had made so that I could have my mid-day meals, this now meant that I was back to sandwiches again. Mum wrote to the Stanmore Head, a Mr. Lovell. Mum had known his brother, who lived in Deane Down Drove in Littleton. I don't know what happened, but Mum then wrote to the Education Department of the HCC and after some while they said I could go to Stanmore after the summer holiday.

I started school at Stanmore in September 1939 just after the war was declared. When I again arrived, this time on my own, it was to Mr. Lovell's study. He did not seem too pleased to see me. I always felt that he didn't like me very much. I was taken to the first year class, which was in the main hall. It was a mixed class of boys and girls and the teacher was a Mrs. Haysome, an older lady, more like the teachers I had been used to at Crawley. There couldn't have been a bigger difference; going from St. Thomas's which was old and rather cramped, to Stanmore, which was new and modern. It also had a large playing field. Sometimes in the hot weather we would have a class under the tree in front of the school. We were allowed to play football and cricket in our dinner hour. We also had swimming lessons. For this we had to go to Bull Drove in Garnier Road. It couldn't really be called a swimming bath because it was only the river with some changing huts and a diving board and was always rather cold.

One of the things I did enjoy was the quite large garden in which all the boys worked for one lesson a week. The garden was all fruit and vegetables. It also had two beehives, which interested me. We were divided up into groups of four or five. We might have to dig, hoe, weed, plant or sow. My ego was enhanced when we were split up into groups because they all wanted me in their group as I was used to gardening and could get the jobs done quicker. On wet days we would have garden theory inside. On such a day the master was giving instructions on the watering of pot plants. He said you should always water pot plants from the bottom. I remember I put my hand up and said "*Please sir, my father doesn't*". I think he could have killed me. Because of the war and "dig for" victory" instruction in gardening for food had become important.

Another class I also enjoyed was woodwork. It was taken by Mr. Aubrey, who helped us make interesting things. I remember making a towel holder with wood and a glass marble. We also made a bedside lamp with a rather attractive twisted stemmas it happened my grandfather, Mum's dad, a joiner in Southampton Docks, was living with us at the time and he encouraged me. I have always enjoyed woodwork every since.

In the second year we all moved up to the class of Miss Vera Hansford. She was a very popular teacher and was liked by everyone, especially the boys. She had a great sense of fun and didn't talk down to us. Besides English and arithmetic she took needlework for the girls and music for all the school, which she always made very interesting. I remember once she played some of the old 78 records of the Mikado. While I was in her class she got married to Roy Portsmouth, the brother of Miss Clarice Portsmouth, who at that time was managing our shop in Winchester. They were married at St. Catherine's Church, Littleton, with many of the children from school attending. Roy was called up into the RAF shortly after the wedding and she came to live with her mother-in-law and sister-in-law at Bercote in the village.

When I was at Stanmore School some bombs were dropped during the day on the St. Cross area of Bushfield Camp. We all had to dive under our desks.

At school in those days the threat of the cane was always there with some of the teachers. Mr. Lovell would come round the classrooms to inspect pupils' work and if he thought it was bad, they would get the cane. I never forgave him on one occasion. He was going to take us for history in the main hall. He hadn't arrived, so one or two of us got the books out ready for the class. When he came in he must have been in a bad mood. He shouted at us *"Who told you to do that?"* and forthwith gave us the cane. So much for using your initiative!

At the start of the spring term in June 1941 I moved school once again, this time to Peter Symonds. I have never been quite sure why Mum and Dad wanted me there. I think it may have been because John was there and they liked to treat us both the same. At that time, although Peter Symonds was a grammar school, about two-thirds were scholarship boys and the other third fee paying, so for five guineas a term I found myself at Peter Symonds and I had to have an interview with the Headmaster, Dr. P. T. Freeman. Mum took me in and I remember he asked me several questions. Mum wasn't given to over-praising us, and when he asked me to read something, she said *"He really is not very good at reading"*, or words to that effect. I read the piece he gave me. He then looked at Mum and said *"What's the matter with that?"* So I started the following week.

Looking back I now realise how disrupted my education was at that time, having attended four schools in just over two years.

Once at Peter Symonds it was compulsory to wear a school cap and tie at all times. If seen without by one of the teachers the punishment could be detention. John had all his books supplied by the school because he was a scholarship boy, but because my father paid for me I had to buy all my own, which my Aunt Nell paid for. This meant a trip to Gilberts in The Square. There were three other boys who started at the same time as me. We were put in 3C, a general form. Once again, I was starting at a disadvantage, being a year and a term behind in most of the subjects. I completely missed the grounding. Subjects like Latin and German I never understood first or last. I gave up Latin at the end of the first year, much to Dad's disappointment. He thought it might have been useful if I had gone into horticulture. The only subjects I got on reasonably well with were geography, biology, art and, in spite of my not being very good at English language, I liked English literature. The subjects I was reasonable at were the ones taught by the good teachers. Because of the war a number of the younger teachers were called up and their places taken by older men who had retired and, for the first time at Peter Symonds, one or two women.

Once again the threat of corporal punishment was always there. Looking back now it seems unbelievable that you were chastised not only for bad behaviour, but sometimes for the lack of ability. It was alright, it seemed to me, if you were academic. I remember one teacher, who shall be nameless, who took history. He would set a test on history dates and if you didn't get at least five out of ten you were put over the desk and walloped! One smacked your face with a ruler, one used a plimsoll and another one used, a chair leg believe it or not, which he called his Alsatian. I must say that I never actually saw it used; perhaps it was just a deterrent or a threat.

There must have been at least ten or twelve boys in the village who were going to Peter Symonds at that time. Most of us cycled to and from school. We also came home to dinner at mid-day. It was about two miles up hill and down dale each way. We travelled down Stockbridge Road, along Bereweeke Road to the Andover Road, then down to the Jolly Farmer, along Owens Road and into school. There was a lot less traffic in those days and far less built up than it is today. At Weeke, where the shops are now, there was only Ron Bayton's garage, and Stoney Lane really was a stony lane. Further on, where Manor Close is, was a farmyard, where sometimes we would get held up by the cows being brought in from Teg Down to be milked. If you were late it was no good telling that to the prefects on the gate.

In the morning as we went along Bereweeke Road, the girls from County High School would be walking up. They had been told by their Headteacher, Miss Wright, that they should have nothing to do with us Peters boys. In fact when we went by they were to look down, so when we passed the boys would shout out *"Eyes down"!* On one occasion, during the war, I was cycling along Bereweeke Road with my friend Alan Gill when the air-raid siren went. We had got used to the siren by that time in the war and took very little notice of it. Then we heard a plane coming over quite low to our right. We got the fright of our lives when we saw it pass the end of the road with a stick of bombs dropping out. I have never got off a bike so quickly in my life! We dived under the hedge of what was then Eastacre Private School. When we felt it was all clear to come out we got up and dusted ourselves down, recovered our bikes and went on to school. We heard later that some of the bombs had dropped in the Hyde area of Winchester.

Once at school the first thing would be assembly, taken by Doc Freeman. It would take place in the school hall. This was a very dark room summer and winter because the windows were very high up and they had been blacked out permanently for the duration of the war. With the brick walls it made it rather sombre. When I went back years later with all the blackout gone it seemed a different place. For assembly we would have to line up across the hall, the junior forms at the front, the senior forms at the back. We were not allowed to talk while we were waiting and the prefects would patrol between the lines to make sure that this was carried outdone word and you were banged on the head with a hymn book. On very wet days we would have to go to school by bus, which meant we couldn't go home to dinner and had to take sandwiches, which we had in the hall. I remember that, as we came out, some of the school boarders would be waiting outside to ask whether we had anything left that we hadn't eaten. If it was a wet Friday, I would sometimes go down to the fish and chip shop, get a shillings worth of chips and take them down to the shop in Parchment Street and eat them there.

At the outbreak of the war, Portsmouth Grammar School was evacuated to Winchester. They used the old private Winton House School, which was on the Andover Road. This was not large enough for them so they used Peter Symonds three afternoons a week; Tuesdays, Thursdays and Saturdays. This meant that we could not have schooling on Tuesday and Thursday afternoons. To make up for this, we had to go in on Saturday mornings. We didn't get the afternoon off either, we had Corps; JTC (Junior Training Corps) or ATC (Air Training Corps) on Tuesdays, and sport of some kind either Thursday or Saturday. We usually had cricket in the summer term, football in the autumn term and rugby in the spring term. I really enjoyed the cricket and played every game I could. I also quite liked the football and played when I was asked, but I didn't like rugby, I think because it lacked proper supervision. The aim seemed to be to tear the shirt off of one another's backs. I think the coldest I have ever been in my life was playing on a freezing January day. After the game my hands were so cold I couldn't do the buttons up on my clothes. I had to cycle the two miles home and when I got there I was literally crying with the cold. The experience didn't endear me to the game of rugby. I joined the Cadet Corps and then on to the JTC. I enjoyed this. As the war was on most of the boys joined this or the ATC. We had old Lee Enfield rifles which we drilled with. The school field on a Tuesday afternoon sounded more like the parade ground at the barracks. On wet days we would do map reading and signalling. At the end of term we would sometimes go out on field exercises, either on the golf course, Crab Wood or Stockbridge Down. We also had to take a test called Cert. A. Besides drill, this also included running, walking and PT. I managed to pass first time and was allowed to wear a red star on my arm. In his last year my brother John was a Platoon Sergeant. I always remained a full blown private. Having an older brother at school, I got fed up with teachers saying *"You will never get on like your brother"*. Even after he had left school and had been called up, I remember replying on one occasion *"I haven't got far to go, he's only a private in the Army"*.

In the summer I spent every opportunity I could in the swimming pool. The only problem was that because the war was on, they were not allowed to change the water very often. There were no filters in those days, so the water got rather green and didn't look very inviting. They did use chlorine to keep it hygienic. The chlorine was kept in large carboys in the school passage. I would not consider myself a particularly strong swimmer, but I always enjoyed it, so I joined the Life Saving Club. One of the tests we had to do was to bring up a brick from the bottom of the six foot. The trouble was the bottom was so green it was impossible to see the brick!

One incident I remember concerning Doc Freeman was when some of the boys during the summer holidays were caught scrumping apples behind the Running Horse Pub and were taken to court. Two of the boys, Eddie Gill and Olly Gowing, were at Peter Symonds. They had lots of apples in their own gardens at home. At assembly on the first day back after the holidays Doc said *"I want to see Gill and Gowing outside my office"*. We all thought *"now they're for it"*. They went in fear and trepidation, but when they came back they were smiling all over their faces. Doc had said to them *"I scrumped apples when I was a boy but as long as you're prepared to take the consequences if you get caught get out of my study"* That's what Doc thought of boys taken to court for scrumping.

One of Doc's favourite topics was the modern generation, and that included anybody under 30. Because of the fear of air-raids, the older boys had to do a turn of fire-watching. During term time this would be covered by the boarders, but during the holidays the day boys, who lived reasonably near the school, were enlisted. Each watch would be covered by a teacher and three boys. We would have to put our names down for duty and, as luck would have it, I was drawn with my friend Reg Saint. The watch during the summer holidays was, if I remember rightly, 9.00 p. m. to 7.00 a. m. The teacher did 9.00 till 1. 00, the other boy did 1.00 till 3.00, and Reg and I would do the last four hours together, 3.00 till 7.00. As soon as it began to get light we would wander round the school and the field and watch the wonder of the dawn coming up. Everywhere seemed so quiet compared to the hustle and bustle of the day. It was late in the war and nothing ever happened on these nights. One morning we wandered out of the school and down to the bridge on the Andover Road and stood there and watched the wagons being shunted in the goods yard ready for the coming day. The atmosphere seemed so different to what it would be later in the day.

Over Christmas the Post Office would use the school hall for sorting parcels. This meant no assembly or PT until the end of term. On my last term, with several of my friends, I volunteered to help deliver the post over Christmas. We were interviewed by someone from the Post Office and accepted to work for ten days before Christmas. I was given the round of Andover Road North and Harestock, which I had to do on a Post Office bike twice a day rain or shine. I also had to go out to a couple of cottages at Well House Farm, which was quite a journey on a cold, wet day. In those days the post was still being delivered on Christmas morning. I especially remember enjoying this. Going in early to the sorting office, collecting the mail and delivering and arriving just as the families were waking up to a Christmas Day which would lift the austerity of wartime, if only for one day. There were the greetings of *"Happy Christmas"* and usually a Christmas box. I really enjoyed my ten days working for the Post Office.

During the last couple of years of the war, the school ran a harvest camp on a farm in Brown Candover, a small village which lies between Alresford and Basingstoke. It ran for four weeks of the summer holidays, most boys going for either the first two weeks or the second two weeks. They would sleep in old army bell tents, have their meals in the farm barn, washing was rough, either under a cold tap or in the water trough. The cooking was done by two young ladies who were learning domestic science. They stayed in a caravan in an adjoining field. There would be one or two teachers in charge with two or three prefects. During the day the boys would be sent out to different farms in the area to help get in the harvest. I didn't put my name down to go because at the time I had other commitments, but my friends Alan and Eddie Gill, did. Unfortunately for Alan about a week before he was due to go he fell off his bike and broke his wrist, but fortunately for me I was able to make arrangements to enable me to go and take his place. Eddie, myself and some other boys from the village set off on our bikes on a Sunday afternoon in August 1944 to cycle to Brown Candover. We arrived at the rather lovely old farm and were allocated our tents and given a straw palliasse to sleep on, which is virtually a sack filled with straw. We slept about four or five to a tent with our feet towards the pole in the middle. Eddie and some other boys were in the same tent as I was. We had our meals sitting at a bare table in the barn. We always had burnt porridge for breakfast! After breakfast we were put in the charge of a prefect, who had to take us on our bikes to the farm where we had to work. We were the smallest group, four of us including the prefect. We arrived at the farm of Mrs. Andrea, which was quite small. Her husband also owned a much bigger farm to which a larger number of boys went, including Eddie. We went into the field where they were bringing in the corn with horse and cart and also a tractor. They were building ricks in the corner of the field, where the prefect went to help. Myself and the other two boys were put in a field where the corn had been cut but the sheaves had not been stood up into stooks. We were given this job to do. Being a country boy, which the other two were not, I had done this job many times. I showed them the way I had been taught and we had the job done in no time. I think the foreman was surprised at how quickly we had got the job done. We then went on and helped pitch the sheaves and load the cart. It was tiring work, and by the time we had cycled back to camp and had our meal it was quite late, so we were soon in our tents and asleep. I really enjoyed the work because for some time I had made up my mind that I was going to be a farmer. The four of us had a surprise towards the end of the second week. Mrs. Andrea was so pleased with us and the work we had done that she invited us to tea. We were shown into the dining room of the big house, where she was waiting for us. On the table there were sandwiches, cakes etc. , the likes of which we hadn't seen for some time because of the rationing. She spent most of the time talking to the prefect, which left the three of us to get tucked into the food. On the last night the teachers and two student cooks went down to the pub for a drink. While they were away, some of the boys moved the students' caravan from the top of the field to the bottom. When the cooks came back in the dark they couldn't find it! Nothing was said the next morning – perhaps the teachers had a guilty conscience. We emptied the straw out of our beds, had our breakfast and were off home, having had a great time and experience.

At assembly one morning in October 1943, Doc said that the Farm Institute at Sparsholt needed help to pick up the potato crop. As this meant time off from school and out in the open air, and on a farm, I was one of the first to volunteer. It also had to be boys who lived near, as we had to use our own transport to get there. When we arrived we were taken out into the field where a potato spinner, pulled by a tractor, was going down the ridges throwing out the potatoes on to the top of the ground in rows. We had to follow picking up the potatoes and putting them into sacks. These were then taken to the potato clamp. It was a back-breaking job and towards the end of the day we were feeling worn out. Some of the boys, to save having to pick them up, just trod the potatoes into the soft earth, but the farm foreman was up to this. When the field was finished he got a harrow and went over the whole field, which brought all the potatoes to the top. We were then sent back to the field to finish the job.

I joined the newly formed photographic club, where we started to develop our own photo's. This did not last long, however, for two reasons because of the war, film was difficult to get hold of and we were turned out of the physics lab because we made too much mess with our developing.

My time at Peters was a bit like the curate's egg. My school report always said *"Could have done better"* and I never thought I was ever going to be an academic. I was unlucky, perhaps, because the war was on, but perhaps if I had been properly motivated I might have done better. It left me with my confidence rather dented. Against Doc's advice, I left without any real qualifications at Christmas 1944. John, who had left school a couple of years before me and had been working on the nursery, was called up into the Army. This left Dad and Grandad to work the nursery and the market garden on their own, unable to get any help. Although I had made up my mind I wanted to be a farmer, I said I would work with Dad and Grandad for 18 months until I was called up and then, when the war was over, I would try to get into farming. But this is not quite how things turned out.

If a man finds himself with a loaf of bread in both hands,
He should exchange one loaf for some flowers,
Since the loaf feeds the body indeed,
But flowers feed the soul.
Mohammed

Old king Alfred bus OU 1704 – our transport to and from Crawley school

Anne, myself and John

Wedding of our popular teacher Vera Hansford to Roy Portsmouth at St Catherine's church, Littleton

John in his cadet corps uniform at Peter Symonds School

Tape 5
Growing-up

When I look back on my childhood, growing up on the nursery in the village of Littleton, I realise how lucky I was and the amount of freedom I had. On the nursery there was always something going on. Next door was the recreation ground, where some friends could always be found to play with and, as we got older, there were open fields around us where we could wander; no-one seemed to mind. We didn't have any of the modern electronic entertainment the children have today, only the wireless and Children's Hour, with Uncle Mac, Uncle David and Toy Town. Different seasons of the year provided different interests, like conkers in the autumn, sledging and carol singing in the winter, birds nesting in the spring, long summer holidays spent in the hay and harvest fields. The rec. was far more interesting to us boys than the short mown grass is today. In the long grass at the top and bottom of the field skylarks nests could be found. We watched them drop from the sky some distance from the nest and then run along the ground towards us and eventually find the nest. The very old hedge, which ran up the far side of the field, was much wider than it is now and could hide a partridge or pheasant's nest. At the very top of the field in the right hand corner were a group of larch trees, where we would have our camp. It was known as "the clump". If I was to say to anyone today who was a child at that time that I would meet them at "the clump", I am sure they would still know exactly where I meant. Further down the hedge was the old crab apple tree. This was great to climb and throw the apples down at our mates below. The hedge was made up mostly of hawthorn, blackthorn, spindle, some hazel and wild cornus, much of it covered in ivy. All ideal for different sorts of birds nests. There was also a holly tree and a field maple tree where sometimes a mistle thrush's nest would be seen in the fork of a branch. On summer nights we went to bed in the daylight to the sound of the peewits calling on the arable field at the back of the nursery.

Although it is breaking the law today, most boys at that time went birds nesting and had their collection of birds eggs. There was always a strict code that you never took more than one egg from a nest. I know it is frowned on today, but although we may not have realised it at the time, we learned a lot about the different birds, their song, their habitat, where they nested, what they ate and the way they flew. I still remember today the spots in the village where you are likely to find different birds. I think the magpies now do far more damage raiding the nests of small birds, than we ever did.

We were encouraged to do things for ourselves. I was given a garden of my own at a very early age. This I managed to look after with a little bit of help from Grandad. When I was very small, I remember, I planted potatoes then kept digging them up to see if they were growing, but soon learnt, like most gardeners, to have more patience. I grew other things, like runner beans, carrots, turnips etc. One evening I was up at the top of the nursery and Mr. Saunders, who was the manager of Hilliers florist shop in Winchester and lived next door, leant over the fence and said *"plant this in your garden"*. It was a small walnut sapling. It flourished, producing very large walnuts. The tree is still there today some 70 years later, now in the garden of a private house.

John was very keen on making a truck out of a set of pram wheels and an old bulb crate. Sometimes they were quite elaborate, with two sets of pram wheels and a steering wheel. He said he wanted to be a bus driver and would spend many hours pushing his truck round the many mown paths on the nursery playing bus drivers. Sitting in it being a passenger or conductor would be our old dog, Michael. John got given the name of *Chuffy*, because he was always chuffing round the nursery.

The field at the back of the nursery, which included what is now the extension to the recreation ground, was farmed by Mr. Andrews of Harestock Farm. He rented it from Mr. Gerald Dean who owned Lower Farm and Littleton Stud. When they were hay-making one day, Mum took us across the field to watch the men building the hayricks. I think she knew most of them. They gathered the hay by raking it into lines across the field with a horse-rake. It would then be gathered with a hay-sweep. It's difficult to describe what this was like, the least I can do is say it was like a large wooden fork with about eight or ten prongs and about eight feet long. This was laid on the ground and pulled along the rows of hay by two horses, one on each side of the sweep. As they went along the rows the hay was gathered up. A wooden back and sides would stop the hay coming off. When full it was driven to the rick, the horses were pulled back, this left a large heap of hay to be pitched on to the elevator, which carried it on to the rick. When we arrived, Mrs. Turner, who lived on Flowerdown, was also there watching the horse going round and round driving the elevator. She got talking to Mum and, in the conversation, said that they had some puppies they wanted a home for. After a certain amount of persuasion and negotiation with Mum and Dad, they let us have a puppy for the princely sum of half a crown. He came with the name of Michael and was our companion, guard, friend, truck passenger, rabbiter and rat catcher for the next 14 years.

The old village hall had a covered veranda along one side. On wet days this was a great place to meet and play different sorts of games. On fine days we would play a game we called 'anti-hi-over', a game I've never heard of anywhere else. It was played with a tennis ball by two teams, one each side of the old cricket pavilion. The ball would be thrown over the pavilion, at the same time shouting 'anti-hi-over'. If one member of the opposite team caught it they would then run round to the other side and the two teams changed from one side of the pavilion to the other and tried to touch a member of the opposite team with the ball. They could even throw it if they wanted. If they were successful, the person who was touched by the ball changed sides. This went on until there was only one person left in the team. This is roughly the game. One other little thing I remember was that if you went to throw the ball over and it rolled back off the roof, you shouted *"pigs-tail"*. Why pigs-tail I do not know.

On long Sunday evenings in the summer we would go for a walk across the fields with Dad. There were lots of hares about then and, if one was coming towards us, Dad would say *"stand still"*. They would come almost right up to us before they realised we were there. When we reached the bottom of Three Maids Hill we would walk up through the beech trees to the crossroads at the top. There, with any luck, would be the Walls ice cream man selling ices to people in their cars who had been out for the day. Dad would buy one each and we would take them through the trees to eat them sitting on the grass in one of the paddocks, sometimes looking at the lovely racehorses in the field. We would then wend our way home by a different route.

As we got older we were expected to help with little jobs on the nursery. We had quite a large orchard with many splendid varieties of old apples. These we had to help pick in the autumn. The bulbs which Dad bought from Holland came in wooden crates. These were cut in half and used for storing apples in. We then had to put the apples gently into the crates. *"Treat them like eggs"*, Grandad would say. The crates of apples were then stored in the loft of Grandad's shed.

At Christmas we had to wire the holly for the holly wreaths. This was often done by all the family sitting round the kitchen table on dark winter evenings by the light of an Aladdin oil lamp. We had no electricity or gas.

A little job we quite liked doing was making up the wooden seed boxes ready for the bedding plants in the spring. Dad would buy the wood already cut to size. Ends, sides and bottom. These would then have to be nailed together, making very sure you didn't hit the wrong nail! Over the years I did get one or two black thumbs. In the spring we would help prick-out the seedlings into the boxes. It was a bit of a fiddly job. There were usually 54 plants to a box. Asters and salvias were easy, Lobelia was always planted in clumps of three or four, but I think the worst thing we ever had to do was if Grandad wanted to plant out some onions later on. They were like a blade of grass with a long root, which was difficult to negotiate into the hole made by the dibber. Another spring job was helping Grandad plant the potatoes, which we had to help dig in. He was very keen on his potatoes and we used to call him 'The Potato King'. The problem as far as we were concerned was that we could hear the boys on the rec. playing football and cricket and would rather have been out there with them. Grandad knew this, because he liked his sport too. He would set us targets, like so many rows. We would work like mad and when it was done we were off out into the rec. Occasionally we were given money for certain jobs we had done, or tips for delivering. We would then go over the road to the Post Office and Village Store run by Mrs. Maskell, Aunty Bertha to us boys, and buy some sweets. Ten aniseed balls for a halfpenny or a penny for a sherbet dab. Sometimes we would have to get ten Tenners cigarettes for Grandad. Dad smoked Craven A, but they both gave up when the war started.

We boys would find dead stems of old man's beard, the wild clematis, break it into short lengths and try to make it burn like a cigarette. It nearly burnt our throats out. I never wanted to smoke after that!

Sometimes Grandad would take us into the market. In those days it was held in Jewry Street in what used to be the car park behind the Library. It was great fun looking at all the animals, but we got a bit of a fright one day when a bullock got loose and Grandad put us in an empty pen for safety. On one occasion it was snowing and the roads were slippery so we had to walk into Winchester. Grandad tied some old sacking round his boots to stop him slipping up.

We still liked to go on the round with the horse and cart. John drove most of the way, but I was allowed to have a go sometimes. It was a very sad day in 1936 when we came home from school to be told that Joe had gone. The old cart looked very forlorn standing there without the pony. It was one of those lessons you learn early in life if you are a country child that you have to accept that animals do not live forever. That one day they are going to die. You learn that in nature one thing lives off of another and that when they are alive they should be looked after and treated with kindness. Some people today would be quite shocked if I said that my Grandfather taught me how to kill a chicken quickly and humanely when I was only ten years old, but forget that every piece of meat or fish we eat has to be killed. We lived close to nature and the seasons of the year. We all live a very different life today and I don't think I could kill a chicken now. Perhaps I might if I was very hungry. Grandad decided not to get another pony, so he sold the cart. This meant the finish of his round. He did, however, visit some of his very old customers, with eggs etc. on a Saturday morning, finishing up at the shop. He would go off with all he could carry on the bus. To get produce into the shop they had a trade bike with a large carrier on the front. The boy who worked on the nursery would take a load of flowers etc. in every morning except Fridays, when Mr. Hillary, the local coalman, would take a load in on his lorry.

By this time, the shop in Parchment Street was getting quite well established, so there was no need for Grandad to spend time on his round. Dad and Grandad worked hard with long hours, gradually building up their business. The two greenhouses became three, then four, and by 1938, five. They were the old school, and they didn't believe in borrowing to build. They made the money, before investing it back. They advertised the fact that everything sold in the shop was grown on the nursery at Littleton. Dad always loved his job. Being a nurseryman was all he ever wanted to be from the time he had a small greenhouse as a boy in Western Road. The love of plants stayed with him all his life. He was still helping to take cuttings on the nursery well into his 90s. The love of gardening and plants that I have today is mostly due to his encouragement.

Between the wars there were two or three other nurseries in the village; Mr. Saint in South Drive and Mr. Street in North Drive. He, like Grandad, had a horse and cart and a round in Winchester, and also a shop in City Road. There was also Mr. Jones in Hilden Way, but he gave up in the mid-30s. Mr. Hall had a market garden where Rozelle Close is now, and sent some of his produce to Covent Garden. Mr. Bright and Mr. Green had poultry farms in South Drive. Mr. Alexander had a smallholding also in South Drive, with pigs, goats and poultry. His son, Bill, who was also known as Alex, was a pal of my brother John. He had his dad's old car, which he used to drive up and down South Drive and he would give us a ride in it. For petrol we would contribute our pocket money and take the petrol can up to Eve's Stores, later the village Post Office, on the corner of Deane Down Drove. The petrol pump was on the opposite corner where the bus shelter is now. It was hand operated, so you had to pump the handle to fill the canvas the car was nearly clapped out, we spent more time turning that starting handle trying to get it to go than we did riding in it!

Very often on a Sunday we would go over to Sparsholt to the Aunts' for tea. After tea we would go out into the bakehouse, where Uncle Sid and one of the men would be making the dough for Monday's bread. It was made in a machine with a big rotating bowl driven by a little stationary engine. When it was mixed into the required consistency the bowl was stopped, turned on to its side and as the dough came out, one of the men would grab an armful while Uncle Sid cut it into a big lump with a knife. It would then be put into wooden bins and allowed to rise overnight. Uncle Sid was always pulling our legs about something. He would say *"Do you know there is snow under the yew tree in Littleton churchyard all the year round?"*. We would go and have a look, and there was a gravestone with the name Snow on it. We would only be caught once! He was very fond of putting his floury hands into our hair, so that when Aunt Nell came along she would say *"Sid, what have you been doing to these boys?"*.

Sometimes during the summer holiday I would go and stay for a week under the care of Aunt Elsie, Mum's sister. She worked in the bakehouse making the cakes. My mouth still waters when I remember the cream buns, still warm. The wonderful smell of baking bread wafted up through my bedroom window when I awoke in the morning. Occasionally my cousin, David Stockwell, would be staying with his grandparents, Uncle Sid and Aunt Alice, in Redthorne, just down the road. We would play together, investigating the van shed or the hayloft and would pretend an old cart was all sorts of weird and wonderful things. We would go down to Ham Green and over the downs where there was the remains of an old car and we would also go out with Uncle Frank in the horse-drawn bread van around Sparsholt and Crabwood. As we got older he would let us deliver the bread to some of the houses, but not to the posh ones. Uncle Frank was not a bit like his brother, Sid. He always seemed a bit sombre, but his wife, Aunt Ti, was a really lovely lady. She was a great sport and we kids were very fond of her. Uncle Frank always seemed to have a mystery about him. I think it must have been a drink problem. Dad said his horse stopped automatically at all the pubs, but it always knew its way home. He died quite young; I think it was what they called DTs.

Just after Christmas one year, when we were much older, Aunt Nell rang up to ask John and myself if we could help with the delivery of the bread, as over half of their staff was off with the 'flu. We helped for about a week, delivering around Littleton and Crawley.

All the delivering for the nursery and the shop was done by a boy on a trade bike. This would be mostly around Winchester. One year, I think it was 1938, it snowed just before Christmas, which made it tricky to ride a trade bike with a load in front, so we went into the shop and walked around the town with the deliveries, most of which seemed to be bowls of hyacinths, cyclamen or azaleas. Delivering flowers at Christmas is a lovely thing to do. When you go to the front door and ring the bell, the expression on people's faces when they see a present of flowers is always one of surprise and joy.

A great Christmas treat for us was going to the pantomime in the Guildhall with Granny and Grandad. We would go on a Friday night, no school the next day, and we'd have the front middle seats in the back balcony. I don't know how Grandad managed that; he must have booked very early. One year it was a great excitement trying to pick out a girl in the cast who he knew. When we came out it would seem very late to us and there would always be a taxi waiting to take us home.

In February in the late 1930s, after a very wet winter, something happened which created an extra adventure for the village boys. The field on the corner of Andover Road at the bottom of Three Maids Hill, flooded. It was caused by a spring which appeared under the old walnut tree across the field at the back of the nursery. There was a culvert under the Andover Road to let the water through so that it could flow across the fields to the river at Headbourne Worthy, but it wasn't large enough to take all the water, so a lake built up. Grandad said that the old locals said it happened about every 50 years, but it has happened three times in my lifetime. We found a very large crate in one of the sheds and a couple of old oil drums which we strapped into it. It was a bit of a struggle, but we pulled it across the ploughed field to the floods, which by now had created quite a deep lake. We floated our raft, which wasn't very stable, but we somehow managed to stay on. Looking back now I realise how dangerous it was, because the water was quite deep.

Some 50 years later when they were talking about building the Sir John Moore barracks, a meeting was held between the Army and village to discuss the matter and display the plans. There was quite a lot of opposition to it at the time and the meeting got quite heated. I pointed out to the Army representative that where they planned to have their firing range and the entrance to the barracks, I had boated as a boy. I think they thought I was just a village yokel out to cause trouble. When the barracks were being built I did, however, have a visit from a surveyor who had a record of what I had said at the meeting. He said that as far as they were concerned they couldn't find any sign of water. A few years later, when the barracks was up and running, I came home from work one evening and the local news was on the TV. I wasn't actually watching, but I pricked up my ears when I heard them say a water main had burst at the entrance to the Sir John Moore barracks in Winchester. I must say, I had a little laugh to myself. So much for developers listening to local knowledge, even if it was from a yokel. The lake appeared, even bigger the contractors had done away with the culvert under the Andover Road when they built the entrance. The army could not use the range or the entrance for about two or three months. The level of the entrance road had to be raised about ten feet to prevent the reoccurrence, costing quite a large amount of money. I know I shouldn't say it, but I did tell them. I expect one day in about 50 years' time, the range will again get flooded.

Because of Dad's job, which meant he had to be on the nursery looking after the plants, watering etc. , for 365 days of the year, going on holiday as a family was out of the question. To solve the problem, Dad would buy what they called an 'away ticket' for a week. This enabled us to travel on the train a certain distance every day of the week to certain places. We nearly always went to Bournemouth and spent the day on the beach. It also meant Dad could do his watering etc. and leave Grandad and a boy to look after the greenhouses for the rest of the day. One lovely holiday we had I do remember was the time when Granny took John and me to Aunt Flo's, Dad's sister who lived at Walton on Thames. I must have been about seven. Uncle Doug was Aunt Flo's husband and was manager of Walton on Thames Gas Works. He always seemed a very happy man, one of those people who believed life was to be lived. He took us round the Gas Works, which was very interesting to us small boys. We also went to London Zoo and to Windsor Castle. I don't think my cousin Bill was quite old enough to go with us. We also enjoyed going down to the River Thames watching the boats in and out of the lochs. When Uncle Doug retired he came to live at a house called Winton, which was at the top of a long drive off of North Drive. They had a large paddock in front where my cousin Bill had his own cricket pitch. This has all now been built over.

One day in September 1937 we came home from school to be told by Dad that Mum wasn't very well and that we would have to have our tea and stay the night with Granny and Grandad. We awoke on the morning of 22nd September to be told we had a baby sister. Granny and Grandad seemed very pleased, as it was their first granddaughter. When we went off to school I wanted to tell everyone, but John said *"Don't tell anyone"*. I don't know why, perhaps he just felt embarrassed; I don't think he was jealous. When we got home and went to visit our new baby sister Anne, the first thing Mum said was *"What did they say at school?"*. Having a new baby sister meant that things were never quite the same again. By the spring of 1938 Mum started to suffer with her nerves. Today I think they would call it depression. By the end of the summer, Mum was so bad that Dad arranged for her to go to a private nursing home in Hove. Anne went to stay with Mum's brother and wife Aunt Madge and family in Southampton. John and I went to live with Granny and Grandad. I realise now that this was quite a task to take on at their time of life as they were both over 70. I was quite happy living with them. Although they never showed a lot of affection, we somehow knew they loved us and we loved them.

In the early 1990s the Hampshire WI appealed for memories of the days gone by in Hampshire. As a tribute to my grandmother I submitted a piece which was called "The rock on which our family was built". This was published in 1994 with many other folks' accounts of times gone by in a book by the Hampshire WI entitled "Hampshire In Living Memory".

A Victorian Grandmother

Granny was a tall upright lady generally dressed in black with a lace neckpiece which nearly always came up to her chin, and her hair was drawn back to form a bun. When she went out she would wear a tall hat with a velvet bow, this she kept on with a hat pin, and as a small boy I was always frightened she would stick it through her head. Queen Victoria had been on the throne thirty years when Granny was born into a small family butchery business right on the county border at Emsworth, and that is where she grew up. When she married Grandad they came to Winchester to live as he was a soldier serving in the Rifle Brigade. Grandad was discharged from the Army after the Boar War as medically unfit – due to rheumatism – and Granny was told she would have to support him for the rest of his life, and at that time she also had a family of three small children, and to keep them they bought a small shop in Western Road, Winchester. This she ran until 1916 as by that time Grandad had recovered enough from the rheumatics to have set up a small-holding and market garden in the nearby village of Littleton. A new house was built on the land in 1916 where she started a new life. Although she had left school when she was only 12 years old, she kept the business books and accounts in a very fair hand. Her family butchery background came in very useful as Grandad killed a pig once a fortnight and also kept chickens, turkeys and ducks, all of which were prepared and dressed by Granny for him to sell from his pony and cart on his round in Winchester. She also made wonderful sausages from an old family recipe.

Granny lived by the clock, up at 7. 00am, dinner at 12. 30pm, tea at 4. 30pm, supper at 9. 00pm, bed at 10. 00pm and woe betide Grandad if he was late for his meal. Diets were not heard of in those days and they believed in hard work and plenty of food, a large proportion of which they produced themselves. There was always bacon for breakfast, a large meal with pudding for dinner, tea was bread and butter and jam and usually a fruit cake and supper was sometimes soup and perhaps something which had been left over from dinner.

After the midday meal when things were cleared away and washed up, Granny would disappear upstairs to wash and change into her afternoon frock. We were very often invited to tea and I remember standing on a chair at the kitchen sink to wash our hands, we also had to brush our hair and "quiff" as Grandad called it.

If we were ill in bed with the usual childhood illnesses, Granny would always come and read to us in the afternoon. With us boys she might have been strict but she was always kind.

Whatever the weather she could be found at Evensong in our little village church on a Sunday evening. The Church was quite a walk from her house and I can remember the Rector saying as she walked into church on a very wet and windy night *"Brave woman"*.

She served on the Parochial Church Council and was a member of the Mothers Union and a Founder Member of the village W. I. , formed in 1924. During the Second World War she ran and collected the National Savings for the village, she organised the knitting of garments for the troops (my brother and I had to learn to knit scarves) and a family of blind evacuees also lived with her for a time.

I can never remember her sitting doing nothing as she was always reading or knitting and in her later years when she could no longer get to church she liked to listen to the services and hymn singing on the radio. Granny lived to the great age of 92 and now I am older I realise my Victorian Granny was the rock on which our family was built, she was always there.

* * * * *

Mum was away for about eight months until early summer 1939, when we were once more back together as a family with our little sister. Mum had a young girl from the village, Mary Ecclestone, as nursemaid for a short time. Her father was the keeper for Gerald Deane who owned Lower Farm and Littleton Stud. He invited us to see the young pheasants in the field penned out with the old hen that had hatched them out. Another treat was when we were invited up to the Stud to see the very young foals with their mothers in the boxes. Those were the heydays of Littleton Stud between the wars, when Lord Astor kept all his breeding mares there. We also saw the stallions as well. I seem to remember some of the names, like Pay-up, Field Trial and Early School.

One day my friend, Bob, greeted me with the news that they were leaving Littleton and were going to live in London. His mum had been brought up in Sparsholt, but his dad was a Londoner and he couldn't settle in the country. Bob was just the opposite; he hated the idea of leaving Littleton. I can still see his face now when he left in the furniture van. When he wrote he said how much he missed the countryside, but his prayers were answered. A few years later when the war broke out in 1939 he came back to live with his aunt in Sparsholt because of the blitz. An old country saying comes to mind. "You can take the boy out of the country, but you can't take the country out of the boy."

Considering its size, there were quite a lot of children in the village and on Flowerdown, so we were able to make lots of friends. Sometimes Mum and Dad would go to the dances on Flowerdown. We would then have to stay overnight with the Scott family who lived in the first house inside Flowerdown gate. As we got older, Mum and Dad would go to the whist drive in the village hall. As it was just over the hedge from our bedroom window, we would be told to go to bed on time. We would be given a whistle to blow if we wanted them. All went well for some time until one night we decided to help ourselves to some seaside rock which Mum kept in a drawer. Within about half an hour I got a raging toothache. I can still see John now, leaning out of our bedroom window blowing the whistle. Mum came running. I wasn't very popular after that and I didn't get a lot of sympathy.

There were, of course, special occasions. One I can just remember was the Silver Jubilee in 1935. This was a combined celebration between the village and Flowerdown and held on Flowerdown cricket field. The field was surrounded by very high steel wireless pylons. So high that they had a red light on the top which lit up at night to warn low flying aircraft. These flew mainly from Worthy Down. Children's sports seemed to be the main thing on these occasions. Not just who could run the fastest, but games like sack race, egg and spoon, three legged race, wheelbarrow and, of course, tug of war. There was also a competition for a decorated bicycle etc. Tea was in the canteen and club used by the Navy and civilian personnel.

The real occasion of the year to us kids must have been the Flower Show. This was the three village show. One year Sparsholt, one year Crawley and one year Littleton and it was always held on the last Thursday in July. It meant the day off from school, which was popular. When it was held in Littleton, the build up to it was looked forward to with excitement. First the long grass had to be cut and cleared, and then a few days after the marquee would be put up. A couple of days before the actual Show the sound of a steam engine could be heard some distance away. We would run up to the road to see a gleaming show engine coming up the road pulling several wagons behind it. It would turn into the recreation ground with a certain amount of puffing and shoving, as the entrance was much narrower than it is today. Once the showmen had their living van and trailer sorted out, they would put up the roundabout, swinging boats and side-show, ready for the big day.

The classes in the Show for the children would include drawing and writing and two classes which would not be allowed today, wild flowers and grasses. We would scour the fields around looking for as many varieties as possible. One of the best parts of the Show, and I still think it is today, was the morning when everyone was arriving with their exhibits, full of great expectations. We arrived with ours. John had a jam jar with grasses and I had one with wild flowers. I remember that smell in the tent with all the vegetables and, above all, the wonderful scent of the sweet peas, still I think one of my favourite scents. A lot of the exhibitors in those days were professional gardeners from the large houses in the three villages. There were two classes, one for professionals and one for the amateurs, which was called "cottagers' class". Dad showed in the professional class with his tomatoes and cucumbers. The wait seemed endless to us boys while the judges were making their decisions, but even then we had to wait until the marquee was open at two o'clock. Once in, we would be looking to see if there was a coloured sticker on our exhibit, red for first, blue for second and yellow for third. One year we got the double, we both had a red sticker, John for his grasses and mine for the wild flowers. In entering those classes we learned a lot about wild flowers and grasses. During the afternoon roundabouts and swinging boats would be in full swing. I hated the swinging boats; they always made me feel sick. Sports would again be held in the main ring, much the same as the Jubilee. The men's hundred yards and the tug of war always created a lot of interest between the three villages. The WI also had a three village competition, with a shield going to the winner.

One thing that was always popular at village shows and fetes in those days was bowling for the pig. This consisted of a board with holes in it with different numbers over them. You then bowled a wooden ball along the ground and if it went through the hole, you scored that number. Participants would have three bowls each. The small pig always created great interest and would be kept in a small pen of hurdles nearby. In the mid-30s, Crawley dropped out and then it became a two village show, Sparsholt and Littleton, which kept going until 1939. An interesting fact that Grandad told me was that in the early days of the Show the committee meeting would be held in the village where the Show was to be held that year. Because there was no transport at that time they had to walk, so the meetings were always held at the time of the full moon to light their way.

Coming home from school one day in 1938 we wondered why all the men of the village were up at the top of the rec. near the tennis courts digging holes. When we arrived we discovered that they were in fact digging trenches in a zigzag. They said there might be a war with Germany. We boys jumped into the trenches and helped with the digging. As we know now, Mr. Chamberlain then came home from Germany with his little piece of paper. The trenches were left as they were for the next 20 years before they were eventually filled in. I can never quite work out what the thinking was. Perhaps the zigzag trenches were dug like that because many of the men had been in the First World War, but why at the top of the rec. I have never worked outfit would have been a long way to have run if there had been an air raid.

In the summer holidays of 1938, Aunt Win asked if I would like to go on holiday with them and Cousin David for a fortnight to Sandown. I think besides giving me a holiday, I would be good company for David, as he was an only child. We had a great time staying in a boarding house, like so many holidays at that time. David's dad, Uncle Lou, who was my Godfather, made me have my hair cut much shorter than I was used to. It must have been a good summer, as we spent most of the time on the beach and in the water, where we both learnt to swim. I remember going on the train from Sandown to Ventnor through the tunnel in the hill, which is now closed. I must have behaved myself because next year, 1939, I went with them again, this time to Weymouth. This was to be the last holiday before the war. No more holidays for a number of years.

Children need love
Especially when they don't deserve it
Anon

The greenhouses in 1935 with Grandad, Wally Merwood and Dad. This photo was hung up in the Parchment Street shop to show the nursery at Littleton where all the produce was grown

The church of St Catherine, Littleton

Six or seven years ago this photo came out of the blue when a lady came up to me at the village show and said that when she was a girl she used to visit my grandmother and she had a photo which she thought was of granny with uncle Fred, aunt Flo and Dad and would I like it. Imagine my surprise when she arrived with it and I discovered that it wasn't dad and his brother and sister but John, Bill and myself with Granny taken about 1934

The old show in the village hall about 1930

The British Legion 1937

Tape 6
The War Years

I was an 11 year old boy when the Second World War was declared on 3rd September 1939 and although I can remember it happening, I can't recall very much about the actual day. Mum and Dad must have been indoors listening to the radio. I know we were playing with John's truck around the nursery. We were not old enough to appreciate the enormity of the situation. It is only now when I look back that I realise how Mum and Dad must have felt, as Dad, not all that long before, had gone through the First World War. But I must say that Dad was always the optimist. He never doubted that we were going to win the war. I remember getting quite upset one day when I overheard two ladies in the village being very pessimistic.

The first thing that happened was that we were all issued with a gas mask in a brown box, which we were told we had to take with us everywhere we went. We had to adjust the thing properly, but they weren't very pleasant to wear because they had a very rubbery smell and the visor would steam up, making it difficult to see. It was a blessing that they never had to be used.

Every village and town had its ARP, Air Raid Precaution Wardens. Among their jobs was to make sure that everyone blacked out their house properly. We were not even allowed to show a chink of light. One of the favourite warden sayings, I remember, was *"Put that light out"*.

For the first few months of the war, life went on much the same. I went to Stanmore for school, and in the village the only real difference was the blind evacuees from Southampton. As there was no school in Littleton, the authorities decided to use the village for blind people. Granny and Grandad had a blind family billeted with them, Mr. and Mrs. Hatch and their two daughters. It was Mr. Hatch who was blind. They only stayed a few months, as they found a house in Crawley to live in, where they lived for many years. They never did go back to Southampton. Some of their descendants still live in the area.

One other thing that happened was the creation of allotments at the top of the recreation ground. Anyone who wanted an allotment could have one, as 'dig for victory' was the slogan at the time. As most of the site was meadow grass, it was a long and laborious job double-digging the plots of 5 and 10 rods. They had to be trenched, cutting the turf off the top and tipping it upside-down into the bottom of the trench. Most of the plots were used to grow potatoes, which were to feed the family and also the pigs in the sty at the bottom of the garden. Keeping a pig became popular again. Pig clubs were formed and through these you were able to get coupons for pig food, but the bacon ration had to be forfeited. When it came time for the pigs to be killed they would be sent off to Harris' bacon factory in Eastleigh. A few weeks later a side of bacon would arrive back. The bacon factory would keep the other half. The offal would have been collected from the factory when the pig was killed.

We were told that if there was an air raid the safest place, if you didn't have a shelter, was the centre of the house. When the air raid siren went for the first time, we all rushed to the bathroom, which was the centre of the bungalow, and sat there on the edge of the bath with just a candle for light, not knowing what was going to happen. After about 20 minutes the all-clear went. I think it must have been a false alarm. After that, Dad decided to dig a shelter in the garden near the back door. It consisted of a hole about 10' long and 4' wide and 6' deep. The roof was made of railway sleepers and corrugated iron, with the chalk and soil which had been dug out put on top. An L-shaped entrance down a ladder was made at one end. Dad must have got the idea having served in the trenches during the First World War. I think it would have been quite safe, except if it had a direct hit.

During the winter of 1939/40 nothing much seemed to happen and life went on much the same. It was not until the summer of 1940, when the daylight raids on Portsmouth and Southampton started, that life began to change. Dad had joined the Rescue Squad which had been formed in the village. All it consisted of was a car and trailer, builders' tools – picks, shovels etc. - and a ladder. One weekend they had to go to Portsmouth after a rather nasty raid. When they came home, Dad seemed a bit disappointed as all they had been asked to do was clear some rubble from the road. It also meant that Dad had to leave the nursery, with just Grandad to look after it, for two or three days.

The Local Defence Volunteers, later to become the Home Guard, had just been formed, so Dad decided to leave the Rescue Squad and join the Home Guard, where he felt he could be of more use. I think Dad quite enjoyed his time in the Home Guard, and when 'Dad's Army' came on the television he loved it, and said it was a little bit like that. Dad kept his rifle in the corner of our bedroom and the ammunition in Mum's dressing table. He was very disappointed once when a German plane came over quite low and he didn't have his rifle with him so that he could have had a pot shot at it! He was actually a very good shot, having been a marksman during the First World War and always enjoyed the days firing on the range at Barton Stacey. He also represented the Platoon in shooting competitions against different villages' Home Guard Platoons. The Home Guard took over part of the village hall, using the committee room as the command post and the gents' cloakroom for an office. On one occasion a bullet got fired through the ceiling of the committee room! At the highest point of the village, off Manor Lane, they had an old shepherd's hut which they used for an observation post, keeping a look out for parachutists. This was manned every night. Dad would be on duty every eight or nine nights and back doing a full day's work the next day. He liked it in the spring and summer, when they listened to the dawn chorus. He said that on a clear moonlit night the cuckoo would call all night. On the rec. they had a small Nissan hut where they kept all their ammunition. The outline of the footings can still be seen today. Sometimes they would give a demonstration of their training to the rest of the village. A cadet corps was formed for the boys. Mr. Shepherd, second in command of the village Home Guard, was in charge, with my brother John, who was a sergeant in the school Junior Training Corps, second in command. We had to become what they called 'runners' when they had manoeuvres, taking messages from the command post in the village hall out to different points around the village and we would sleep on the stage in the hall.

When the war finished a large parade was held in Winchester of all the platoons of the district, at which they were officially disbanded. When Dad came home he said the Home Guard were some of the happiest five years of his life, in spite of all the worries of what might have been.

In the summer of 1940 we went and helped with the harvest at Littleton Farm and Stud which was owned by Mr. Gerald Dean. There were three of us boys; John, myself and a school friend, Willy Sandford, whose father was the Stud groom. Willy's and my job was to lead the carthorses from stook to stook.

We would lead the horses up the row of stooks. There would be one man on each side of the cart to pitch the sheaves up and on the cart to load them would be another man. We had to stop at each stook, then on to the next. We had to make sure the horse stopped and started smoothly, otherwise the man on the cart could fall over. If we happened to start off with a jolt they would shout and swear at us boys, the sort of language I never heard at home. There never seemed to be any hard feelings, I think it was just normal for them. Because he was older, John was given the job of driving the cart from the field to the ricks to be unloaded. I think his experience of driving the pony and cart several years before came in handy. He had to be careful not to hit the corner of the ricks as he brought the load in. Once unloaded, he would drive the empty cart back to the field. Several of the fields were in the paddocks which belonged to the Stud and had been ploughed up to produce food because of the war. One of them was used to produce potatoes, but it also produced a fantastic crop of mushrooms. The ground looked white. Many folk from the village turned up to pick them.

As the number of racehorses lessened and many of the paddocks were ploughed up, some of the men transferred from the Stud to the farm. The Stud isolation boxes and the Blackness Stables were also taken over by the farm. The isolation boxes in Drovers' Way were taken over in the spring of 1940 to stable the farm horses after a disastrous fire destroyed most of the old farm buildings at Lower Farm. They were able to save all the farm horses, but some 50 pigs were burnt to death. The fire was first discovered at 8.30 in the evening of 30th March by Freddie Windibank, the farm tractor driver. You could see the glow in the sky from our bedroom window when we went to bed, but we didn't know what the cause was. It wasn't until the next morning that the word got round. We lads were off like a shot on our bikes. When we got to the Stud entrance we saw the fire hoses, which stretched from there to Lower Farm, about half a mile. They had to be used because all the water in the farm pond was soon used up. When we arrived the firemen were still there damping down. There were dead pigs everywhere and we were soon told to clear off. The fire was thought to have started in the tractor shed.

One lovely hot summer day we were out harvesting in the middle of a large 45 acre field called White Lines when the air raid siren went. We were told to run and get in the air raid shelter at one of the farm cottages. I don't know what danger they thought there was out in the middle of a field. This must have been at the time of the Battle of Britain. Perhaps they thought we were going to be machine-gunned. After a while we went back to the field and carried on.

The air raid siren for Littleton was on Flowerdown. Before the outbreak of war it would sound every weekday morning at 8 o'clock. I cannot recall why, perhaps it was as an alarm clock for the staff on Flowerdown.

On 25th September 1940 there had been a daylight raid on Southampton. The aircraft guns had been firing, but sometimes the shells didn't explode in the air and would just travel on. These would sometimes pass over Littleton, making a whistling sound as they went over. This day, one dropped in a field at the backbit didn't explode and just made a mound of soil like a big molehill. About 9 o'clock the same evening the siren had gone, but we carried on eating our supper of cheese and pickled onions, when we heard the whistling noise again, but this time followed by a large explosion and then another. We suddenly realised it was a bomb. Mum, John and I dived under the table, but Dad rushed into the bedroom to get Anne. There were about 10 bombs altogether. First they started to get nearer and then began to get further away, much to our relief. I remember Dad saying "*My God, the glass*", thinking of his greenhouse. Somehow, even in adversity, Dad always seemed to see the humorous side. Afterwards he said we looked like a lot of ostriches with our heads under the table and our backsides sticking out! The first bomb had dropped in the field near the old pumping station; the next near the entrance to Flowerdown off Kennel Lane; the third fell on a bungalow on Flowerdown, which sadly killed Mrs. Winter, whose husband was a sailor on the camp; the next fell in the field at the back of the nursery, which broke about thirty panes of glass; one on a hedge killing a pheasant; the rest in the fields across Three Maids Hill. Some incendiary bombs also fell on the field near Lower Farm, but didn't do any damage. The next day we collected shrapnel from the craters made by the bombs.

Three days later three more large bombs dropped on the Stud paddocks near the top of Three Maids Hill, killing three horses. Ironically they were owned by a German and could not be returned to Germany at the outbreak of war. When these dropped we were in bed asleep. The general feeling in the village was that Littleton and Flowerdown were not intended targets, but the planes were either damaged, caught in the searchlights, or just in a hurry to get home. This was the only time that Littleton had any bombs during the war.

After these incidents we tended to go into the shelter when the siren went. The Gill family, Mrs. Gill and the three boys, would come running down the path to share our shelter every time the siren went, even in the middle of the night. Sometimes if we didn't hear the siren we knew it had gone when we heard the Gills coming down the path.

In the spring of 1941 the raids in Southampton were very heavy and on Good Friday Mum's brother, Uncle Percy, arrived at the nursery with Aunt Madge, Maurice and Gerald in a taxi, with a galvanised bath strapped on the back and with all their worldly goods. A landmine had dropped near their bungalow in Southampton. Grandad Goater, Mum's Dad, was already living with us. He had had enough of working in the docks in Southampton. The bombing had shaken him up. This meant there were 10 of us living in a two bedroom bungalow. We four boys had to sleep in the air raid shelter. As it was the summer we didn't mind. After a couple of months Uncle Percy found a bungalow to rent in the village, intending to go back to Southampton after the war, but they stayed in Littleton and never returned.

By the harvest of 1941 I had got to know many of the men who worked on the farm, including the owner, Mr. Gerald Dean, who was quite a friend of Grandad, in spite of the fact that they had a row when they first met. All the corn would be cut by a binder and tied into sheaves which would then have to be stood up into stooks to dry, about six or eight to a stook. The binder would either be pulled by three horses or by a tractor. It would go round and round the field, the standing corn gradually getting less until there was a small amount left in the middle of the field. As the binder went round, the many rabbits that lived in the corn would move further to the middle. As the middle got less and less, the rabbits would panic and have to make a run for it, when they would either be shot or caught by men and boys with a stick. This may be frowned on today, but it must be remembered that food was short and a rabbit made a good meal. Also, that the rabbits caused a tremendous amount of damage to the young corn. I remember seeing fields with no corn growing within 20 yards of the edge, all eaten by rabbits. It was a case of them or us. When the whole field had been cut, all the rabbits, and sometimes a hare, would be laid out on the ground. Every boy and man would be given a rabbit to take home. Sometimes in a large field there would be well over 100 rabbits. When the field had been cut, we boys would be paid threepence an hour to help the men put the sheaves into stooks.

As we got older we also helped with the loading of the carts. Once I was sitting on the top of a load of sheaves on its way to the rick when the cart hit a large bump. The whole lot slid off, with me sitting on the top!

As I got older I spent more and more of my time on the farm, not just at harvest. I became very fond of the heavy horses. They all had different personalities and I can still remember most of their names. My favourite was Rose, she was a very large shire horse with a placid temperament, but one day she was involved in a rather unusual incident. During the winter, very often when the ground was frozen, the horses would be used to cart the manure from the stockyard out to the field. To do this they would use a flat topped cart, with one horse in the shafts in the cart and another in front called the trace horse. The two horses, one behind the other, would be used to pull the cart, when loaded, out into the field. When it had been emptied the trace horse would be unhitched and tied by its bridle to the back of the cart for the journey back to the yard. On this day, Violet, a smaller horse than Rose, was in the shaft of the cart and Rose was tied on behind when they arrived back at the yard. Something must have startled Rose, as she reared back, at the same time turning the cart and Violet completely over. Violet was kicking about trying to get up, but being fixed to the cart she couldn't. A shout went up, "*Sit on her head*". This kept her quiet until she was released from the shafts none the worse for her ordeal.

As soon as I got home from school I would be up the farm to help feed and groom the horses. Mr. Gerald Dean would always make us welcome. Sometimes he would take us pigeon shooting or ferreting. This was usually done in the winter. Occasionally he would tell us to come up to Littleton House, where we would have to go into the kitchen and help make sandwiches to take with us. There was no such thing as sliced bread then, we had to cut the slices off the loaf before making the sandwiches. I always remember him saying "*Butter the bread on the loaf before you cut the slice*". Good advice. When ready, we would go off in the pony trap pulled by Nobby, a Welsh cob. This was Mr. Dean's form of transport round the farm. Two or three times a year he would have an organised shoot, when we would be beaters, driving the birds towards the guns. When I was older I was allowed to drive Nobby in the trap, which was used to carry the game which had been shot.

During the winter the ricks of corn would have to be thrashed. The thrashing tackle would arrive. This consisted of a steam engine, thrashing drum, a bailer, an elevator and a sleeping hut on wheels, all pulled by the engine. The thrashing drum would be positioned between the ricks and the sheaves pitched on to it from the rick. A roll of small mesh wire would be put round the whole lot to catch the rats that ran out as the rick was being demolished. The farm men would say *"Are you going to bring your dog up to help catch them?"* I would take him, me on my bike with Michael on a piece of string coming along behind. He would jump on to the rick with the men and catch the rats as they ran out, sometimes more than 50 in a day. He was so tired at the end of the day that I had a job to drag him home, but he was always willing to go again the next day. Michael was a wonderful ratter; we never had a rat on the nursery when he was alive. There were so many rats about in those days – they thrived in the corn ricks. I can remember one Boxing morning we took Michael and another friend's dog with us across the fields and we caught 11 rats in one morning.

By this time I had really made up my mind I was going to be a farmer. My idea was that I would go to the Farm Institute at Sparsholt and then get a job on a farm. Sometimes, instead of going up to the farm, I would go to the Stud, where my friend's Dad, Mr. Sandford, was the Stud groom. We would help 'catch up', as they called it, which meant in the winter going out to the paddock to collect the horses and lead them back to the stables. They were never difficult to catch as they would know their supper would be served as soon as they got back. In those days a goat would sometimes be kept at the stables. It would be used to put in with a horse, I think when the horse was sometimes sweating or lonely.

Mr. Sandford had a lovely nanny-goat called Daisy which he bought from Mr. Alexander in South Drive. He was going to use her for milking as well. One day he said he was leaving his job at the Stud, but could not take Daisy with him so he was looking for a home for her. He was willing to sell her for £2. He also said she was going to have a kid. I thought this might be a chance to start my farming experience. When I put the proposal to Dad he wasn't too keen, reminding me that I was still at school with two hours homework every night and that I would have to get up early to milk her before going to school and again when I came home. When I told Grandad what Dad had said, he replied *"Tell Dad that if you find it too much, I will help you out"*, and with good old Grandad's blessing, Dad said it was all right. I think Grandad wanted the goat as much as I did. I went up to Mr. Sandford with my £2 and brought Daisy home and put her into Joe's old stable. I thought I had become a farmer! I had my goat and John had a lot of rabbits (Flemish Giants) which were kept for meat. They were to be our war effort – John his rabbits, mine to be goat's milk. Unfortunately, it didn't quite work out, because Daisy didn't have a kid, and without a kid there was no milk.

I had a school friend, Keith Willis, who lived at the end of South Drive, whose father had a billy-goat. I decided to consult him regarding what the problem might be. He said Daisy was rather old, about 3 ½, to have a first kid, in other words she might have missed the boat. However, in the autumn Daisy paid a visit to Mr. Willis' and was introduced to his billy-goat. For the next five months we lived in hope, until one Sunday afternoon I looked over her stable door and there was proud Daisy with her offspring, two adorable billy-kids. She was a good mum and was soon producing plenty of milk, at her peak up to seven pints a day, more than was required by the kids so I was soon milking her morning and night. Her milk was creamier than cows' milk and made wonderful rice puddings and custard. We had more than we could use and I was soon supplying Granny and one or two other people in the village with milk. The two kids created a lot of fun watching them playing. They would follow me around, even indoors. I knew I wouldn't be able to keep them as they were both billy-kids and the day came when I had to sell them. At that time we had a two wheeled truck which was used on the nursery. I got a big bulb crate and put the kids in it on the truck. John also had some rabbits he didn't want and these he also put in a box on the truck. Our intention was to take them to the market in Winchester. John said *"What are we going to do when we get there?"* Mum said *"It's all right, Austen will do the talking!"* Off we went to market with our truck loaded with our animals. We managed to get the paperwork done without any trouble. I don't think they had goats very often. We sorted them out all right and got them put into their proper places and parked our truck with all the farm cattle lorries. The goats and rabbits all sold for more than we had expected, so we pushed our truck home feeling very pleased with ourselves.

The following year Daisy had two more kids and in the meantime I had bought another goat. I also built up my own small milk round in the village. It soon became evident I was trying to do too much and with school exams coming up I decided to give them up. I didn't have any difficulty selling them, but I kept Daisy in spite of being given a very good offer for her. I pensioned her off and she spent the remaining years of her life keeping the grass short in the paddock.

The most important thing to each of us boys was our bike. It transported us everywhere. It became almost part of us. My first bike was an Elswick, which I had for many years. I learnt to ride down the track on the nursery. To dismount I just leant on the wire round the chicken run. Their main use was to transport us to school every day. We would also ride around the village and the rec. During the holidays we would go as far as surrounding villages, as well as into Winchester to The Lido for swimming. I always took my bike when I was going up to the farm. I think the furthest we ever went was when we went to football at The Dell in Southampton. I'm afraid some of the bikes got very knocked about, mine included, and weren't very road worthy.

During the war the population of Littleton was far less than it is today, even with the people who lived on Flowerdown and Harestock. Like most villages, the war increased the community spirit and there always seemed to be something going on. Most things seemed to be for the war effort. Granny ran the National Savings and Mum and Dad bought us a half a crown stamp every week so that when we had six it was worth fifteen shillings and we were given a Certificate which would increase to one pound in ten years. We did this most of the war years and they came in very useful when I got married just ten years later. Granny also organised a knitting group making garments and scarves etc. for the troops. Even we boys had to learn to knit scarves. In the summer the WI organised a canning day, when the villagers would take their surplus soft fruits to the hall where they had a canning machine. Waste paper could be taken to Eve's Stores shop, where it was sorted in their garage. First aid instruction classes were held by the ARP in the hall. They were taken by Dr. Lowden, a well known Winchester doctor. We boys would sit in the front row taking in all the most gruesome details. I don't think we were that brave, we just couldn't be a coward in front of our friends.

I think many of the WI meetings contained talks on how to make a small amount of food go a long way. I know we enjoyed some of the recipes Mum brought home. One of the problems with food was that there wasn't much variety. We had our own orchard and plenty of apples for most of the year. Although I quite liked apple pie, we had it so often that by the end of the war I said that I never wanted to eat an apple pie again! I am pleased to say that some

60 years later I now eat them and thoroughly enjoy them.

During the war the village Memorial Hall was used nearly every day of the week. Monday night would be the British Legion. Both Dad and Grandad were keen members. The Legion always held a big whist drive and draw every Christmas. The next most important event would be the Armistice parade, which would be held on the Sunday afternoon nearest Armistice Day, 11th November. They would meet at the hall for the parade with all their medals and march through the village with their banner and poppy wreath to the church where the Remembrance Service would be held. A bugler would sound the last post and reveille. The wreath would be laid under the war memorial, which at that time was in the church. After the service they would march back through the village to the hall and the tea. It always interested me that many of the members of the Legion on parade would not be regular attendees at the church, but were drawn on this special occasion because it had so much deep seated meaning for them – memories of comrades and thoughts of those who didn't return. Perhaps like the farm-workers' harvest festival, it meant something special to them.

The Women's Institute would meet on Tuesdays, but during the winter they changed their evenings to afternoons. On Wednesdays a Girls' Club would be held. Vera Portsmouth was the leader, helped by some of the girls' mums. They played netball in the rec. in the summer. Thursday evening would be the whist drive, with Mr. Saint in charge. Several of us teenagers went. There was no messing about, you had to concentrate. If you happened to make a mistake, one of the elders would very soon tell you off. Friday nights would be the Boys' Club. There would be table tennis, a small billiard table, a type of skittles, and boxing. Alan Gill and I nearly always started off with the first bout. If some of the Home Guard were in the hall, they would also join in. Sometimes there would be dancing lessons and the girls would join us. Mr. Chew was the instructor, helped by his wife and Vera Portsmouth. Saturday evenings there would very often be a dance, a good opportunity to try out our quicksteps and quarter turns that we had learnt on the previous evening. We would scrape candle grease on to the floor to try to improve the surface for dancing. Once we put on too much and made it more like an ice rink!

We boys had to organise our own football and cricket. Our goal posts consisted of two posts with some string across the top. For cricket we had to mow our own wickets. The outfield would be long grass. Footballs and cricket balls were difficult to get. The ones we used were very old and battered. We would organise games against boys in other local villages and would cycle to Kings Worthy and Hursley. When the Boys' Club was formed sport became more organised, mainly due to Ted Newman, who ran the club. He lived at number 1 Hollands Close, next door to the rec. Mrs. Newman made our football kit by dyeing our old white shirts green and making the shorts out of black-out material.

Many of the large houses in the district were taken over and used by the military. Early on in the war they were used by the British troops when they returned from Dunkirk. Some of the troops came into the village to the Running Horse and a few came to the dances in the hall. Mum and Dad made friends with two of the soldiers who were in the Engineers in Northwood Park. They would often come home at the weekends. Jeff, who came from Bristol, remained a friend for some time after.

As the war progressed, and the build up to D-Day began, the British troops left to move elsewhere. Northwood and Crawley were then occupied by American troops; Engineers at Northwood and the Medical Corps at Crawley Court. In the village a Friendship Club was formed. This was held in the hall on Sunday afternoons. The idea was to invite the troops. They were entertained to tea with dancing and entertainment. They were very fond of playing darts I remember. Afterwards some of them would be invited by villagers into their homes. We became very friendly with Bob and Roy. I remember Mum saying *"They're only young lads a long way from home"*. They were both interested in music and on a Sunday we would have a musical evening. At that time I had just started to learn the violin. Roy would play this beautifully, with Dad playing the piano. I remember them playing a duet of Dad's favourite piece, the Intermezzo from Cavalleria Rusticana. Bob had a very nice tenor voice and when Vera Portsmouth heard him sing one Sunday afternoon she arranged for him to have singing lessons in Winchester. The song he loved most to sing was The English Rose from Merry England. I always remember something Bob said when asked if he had a girlfriend. His reply was *"The girl I marry will have to be too proud for me to go to work!"* One Sunday the Americans gave a demonstration baseball match on the rec. We tried to show them how to play football, but they kept wanting to pick the ball up. When we tried to show them how to play cricket, they were completely lost.

The American troops started to arrive in 1943 and by 1944 the whole area was full with both British and American troops. There were sometimes reports of clashes between them at pubs and dances. Many of the local roads were widened for the lorries and some were closed completely. One of the carriageways of the Winchester by-pass was closed to park the tanks. The Andover Road from the top of Three Maids Hill to Hill Farm crossroad was closed again for tanks, hidden under the trees. Two of the sheds used for the maintenance of the tanks are still there, just off the main Andover road on the Crawley road.

I was cycling to school one morning with Keith Willis and as we swung out on to the Stockbridge Road two abreast, Keith on the outside, an American lorry came up behind us and hit Keith from behind. He went clean over his handlebars, did a somersault and stood up! He was a very keen horse-rider and had learnt how to fall. The lorry had crushed his bike under the front wheels. It backed off and Keith picked up his squashed bike, put it over his shoulder and said *"I'm not going to school today"* and walked home.

Suddenly one day all the troops disappeared. Everywhere seemed very quiet, almost an eerie atmosphere. Then one night the sky seemed full of planes and on 6th June 1944 we heard D-Day had begun. I shall always remember in the evening we boys were playing cricket on the rec. The American Dakotas were landing on Chilbolton Down. The straps were still hanging out of the side of the plane, left when the airborne troops had bailed out over Normandy. When the bridgehead had been established and the planes could land in Normandy, the Dakotas would bring the wounded back to Chilbolton to be treated at the large American hospital on Stockbridge Down. There is no trace of the hospital to be seen today.

Bob and Roy both survived the war and Bob kept in contact with letters and cards. John's son, Nigel, visited him when he went to America and Bob did make a visit back once with his daughter. I wouldn't have recognised the young lad of about 20 who was now a man in his 60s. My sister Anne still keeps in contact with his daughter.

Grandad enjoyed taking us three grandsons out for the day. Bill, John and myself. A couple of trips I remember were to Horndean and Salisbury. As the war was on and petrol was rationed, most trips had to be either by train or bus.

When we went to Horndean we would go into Winchester by bus and then catch the Petersfield bus. At Petersfield we would then travel on the Portsmouth bus as far as Horndean, where Grandad had been born and brought up and where his half sister still lived. We visited her and then he took us on across the fields to Rowlands Castle, showing us the farm where he started work as a 12 year old boy and told us what life was like for a boy on the farm at that time. When we went to Salisbury we caught the bus from Winchester to Andover and the bus from there to Salisbury. We went into the Cathedral and then sat in the grounds outside looking up at the amazing spire, eating our sandwiches which Granny had prepared for us. We really enjoyed our trips out with Grandad in the summer holidays.

Of all my memories one of the saddest must have been the day John joined the Army, but that is not the memory I have in mind. We said our goodbyes to John in the morning. It was one of those lovely soft spring days that tell us that winter is at last over, the countryside showing a haze of green shoots and everything looking tranquil and peaceful. Reality was in fact far from this. The date was the 6th April 1944 when the countryside around the village was teeming with troops and military armour, both British and American, preparing for D-Day, which was to be exactly two months later. As it was the first day of the Easter school holidays, we boys of the village were a bit like young colts that had been just let out on to fresh green pastures. One of the great interests for village boys was birds nesting, so with this in mind some of the boys decided to go to Farley Mount. We had been warned at school not to go there, because the American troops were using it for tank training. However, boys will be boys and five boys, John Greaves, Peter and John Guppy, Bill Snow and Johnny Denham, set off on three bicycles. Once there, they started to explore, when one of the younger boys picked up an unexploded grenade. The older boys shouted at him to put it down, but the warning was too late. The grenade exploded, killing two boys, seriously injuring one and less seriously injuring the other. One of the boys killed was John Greaves, the other killed was Peter Guppy and his brother seriously injured. The other boy injured was my cousin Bill Snow. As was the custom in those times, the body was laid out in the coffin in the front room of their house and people would pay their respects by going to the house and viewing the deceased. We boys were expected to do the same and it was my first experience of seeing anyone dead. More than 60 years later I can still remember the effect on the village community. As Dad was the local nurseryman and florist, we had to help him well into the night preparing wreathes and flowers for the funeral. This was a very sad occasion with the two small coffins carried up the Church path between walls of flowers held by the village children. All I can recall from the service was the Parson, Rev. Tanner, telling us that our bodies were only the tents in which we lived. The boys were laid to rest in the tranquil village cemetery among the daffodils on a lovely spring day. They were the victims of the consequences of the war just as much as any soldier killed in action. They grew not old as we who were left grow old.

On 4th February 1945 young brother Richard arrived in this world. It was a bit unusual having a brother 17 years younger and an older brother in the Army somewhere on the front line in France or Germany.

Fairly early on in the war Dad, with his usual optimism, bought quite a large Union Jack from Carters shop, which was opposite ours in Parchment Street. He said that as soon as we had won the war we would put the flag up the pole which we used for our wireless aerial. It was put away in a drawer and we all knew where it was kept.

During the spring of 1945 and as the allied troops, my brother included, advanced, we spent a lot of time listening to their progress on the radio. We didn't know it at the time, but John was among the first British troops to reach the Rhine. He was a Sergeant in the Highland Light Infantry, having never been to Scotland in his life! On the evening of 7th May I was at home on my own. Mum was out with baby Richard and Dad was in the hall with the British Legion. I was listening to the radio, most likely the ITMA show, when it was announced that hostilities with Germany would cease the following day. I rushed to the drawer, got out the flag and ran it up the pole. Dad was in the hall from where he could see it and all the men came out. I was able to tell them the news.

That evening it was announced that the following days, 8th and 9th May, would be public holidays. It was decided that a village celebration would be held in the hall and the rec. on 9th May. On the morning of 8th May, everyone sat round the wireless to hear officially that peace was declared. I was a 17 year old, and all my teenage years had been wartime. In fact I could hardly remember what peace was like. The main thrust of our lives had been to win the war. As it happened, 9th May was to be Grandad's 80th birthday, but he spent most of the day before going round the village collecting money and informing everyone about the celebrations.

On the evening of 8th May, at about 8 o'clock, a group of us village boys decided to walk into Winchester to join in the celebrations. The streets were flooded with people, no-one wanted to be indoors. We went right down the town where there were hundreds of people in The Broadway dancing around King Alfred's statue. At about midnight we started to make for home, although there were still a large number of people about, everyone talking to everyone. There were no strangers. Once out of the City we started to make quicker progress home. When we got as far as Harestock corner on the Stockbridge Road – it must have been 2 o'clock or 3 o'clock in the morning – I have a memory I shall never forget. We stopped to hear the nightingale singing in the tree above us. We had our own Berkeley Square. We stayed for some time, before wandering on home, getting into bed just before daybreak.

The morning of 9th May we spent collecting wood and building a bonfire on the rec. The celebrations started in the afternoon with a comic cricket match. Harry Edwards dressed up as W. G. Grace, with a top hat and a beard made out of plumbers' hemp. George Gregory wearing a bowler hat, a rather rotund figure, was his bat-man. He accompanied Harry to the wickets carrying two armfuls of bats. Harry proceeded to try them all, before choosing a suitable one. Many players were dressed up. The result of the game didn't matter. Dear Ike Hillier, who had been a cricketer and was umpire, unfortunately didn't have a great sense of humour, and kept spoiling things by giving players out. Tea was taken in the hall and on the veranda, most likely organised by the Women's Institute. After tea there were games and sports for the children. The bonfire was lit as soon as darkness fell. There were no fireworks available then, but the Home Guard found some thunder flashes which they would no longer require for training, and let them off. The day was finished off with dancing in the hall, with Uncle Fred on the piano and Mr. Hillary with his big drum. Like every occasion during these times, it was finished by singing the National Anthem. The whole event was repeated again in August, when hostilities ceased against Japan.

Littleton lost four of its residents due to the war. Mr. Sinclair, who lived at Bowmore, was lost serving in the Merchant Navy; Mrs. Winter was killed on Flowerdown; and the two boys, John Greaves who lived at Charlton and Peter Guppy of 2 Highfield Villas. Unfortunately, unlike the five men of the village who died in the First World War, there is no memorial to them. After the war it was several years before things began to return to normal.

Everyone suddenly burst out singing
And I was filled with such delight
As prisoned birds must find in freedom
Winging wildly across the white
Orchards and dark-green fields, on,
on and out of sight

Siegfried Sassoon
(words for the memorial sculpture in the New Hall)

Chalkpit Hill 1940 with notice on the right: 'Blind Billeted Here'

Littleton home guard the officer on the left is Jack Denham

Horse binder with men and boys catching the rabbits in the last piece of corn

Small boy sat on the binder with the rabbits, the men and boys would be given one each to take home for rabbit pie

Under 17 boys' club football team. Back row left: myself, Keith Guppy, Geoff Forgham, Cyril Forrester, Leslie Waterman, Eddie Gill, Ted Newman. Front row left: Brian Dunford, Denny Macklin, Gerald Goater, Brian Gill, Geoff Strange. Sitting: John Mason

The family with Roy who was one of the American troops stationed at Crawley court

Myself with Mrs Sinclair (whose husband was killed in the war), Anne and cousin Bill standing in the bomb crater in the field at the back of the nursery 26th September 1941

Grandad, Dad and John, 5 April 1944. The photo was taken the day before John joined the army, I can't help wondering what dad was thinking having been through WW1 himself

Tape 7
Working on the Nursery

I started work on the nursery with Dad and Grandad at Christmas 1944. One of the first jobs I did was to help make the holly wreaths. To do this, Dad had his own method, which we soon learnt. It was one of the first steps in floristry. All the holly wreaths that we made were to be put on graves, not on doors as they are today. Floristry was quite a large part of the business and was a job I had to learn quickly. Most of it would be the making of wreaths, sprays, crosses and floral tributes. In those days people expressed their sympathy with flowers far more than they do now. Sometimes there would be so many tributes that we would have to get Mr. Hillary, with his lorry, to deliver them to the house. If it was a large funeral it could be difficult to find enough flowers, as we were only allowed to grow 10% flowers in the greenhouses and 25% outside, all of the rest had to be used for food production. Most of the villagers at that time would have had quite large gardens and Dad would often buy any surplus flowers and vegetables they might have.

As there hadn't been a boy on the nursery for some time, and Dad had not learnt to drive, to take produce into the shop he asked Horrie Saint, who had a nursery in South Drive, to do the job for him, except on Fridays, when Frank Hillary would take a lorry-load. One of my first jobs in the morning would be to load up the nursery truck with flowers, vegetables and plants and take them down to Horrie's in South Drive. On the nursery there were also certain jobs at certain times of the year. As it was not possible to sterilize soil in those days, and tomatoes do not like being grown in the same soil every year, we had to change all the soil in the greenhouses. This was a winter job which kept us warm, wheeling one barrow-load of soil in, and one out. As most of the greenhouses were used for growing tomatoes (we were not allowed to grow cucumbers, as they were considered of no food value), it was a big job and took up a lot of the winter. Other crops I remember we grew were lettuce and French beans in pots.

One year in one of the houses we had to grow runner beans because all the tomatoes, which were about half grown, were ruined when a sulphur burner, which heated yellow sulphur until it vaporised to control mildew on the tomatoes, caught fire producing an entirely different chemical reaction, killing everything in the greenhouse.

In those days there were no restrictions on the chemicals used. Dad had an old oil stove with a paint tin lid on top into which he poured 35% nicotine to be heated. This produced fumes which killed the aphids. To control whitefly he used cyanide. He would take a spoonful out of the tin and then walk backwards down the greenhouse path just dusting a little out of the spoon as he went. The only protection he had would be an old handkerchief held over his nose. It didn't seem to do him much harm, however, as he lived until he was 94.

As there was a shortage of coal and the amount of coke we could get for the boilers was restricted, only two of the houses were heated for most of the winter, and wood was used to supplement the coke. This would be used during the day and last thing at night the boilers would be stoked with coke to keep them going all night.

When the war finished in 1945, food was still rationed and in short supply and we were encouraged to grow as much food as possible. Because of this I was immediately exempt from National Service in the forces, although I had already registered. I had to stay on the nursery for five years, otherwise I would be called up. There was also a scheme to release members of the services who had worked on the land called "Class B Release". Dad applied for John and he was home within a fortnight, thus showing how important food production was considered at that time.

It was great to have John home. When he left the army we were still teenagers, but we were now young men. We worked together for the next 50 years in partnership, building the business. In all that time we may have had our own ideas and a few disagreements, but we never had anything like a row.

In the spring of 1946 Fred Day, who had been a boy on the nursery in the 1930s, was demobbed from the army and he came to work with us. As Grandad was now in his 80s and suffered with his rheumatics he began to take life a bit easier, although he still liked to keep his chickens and visit one or two of his old customers on a Saturday morning.

Because of the war, Dad had not been able to expand and build any more glass and one of the first things he had to do was to rebuild the oldest greenhouse, which had been built before the First World War and had suffered when the bomb fell in the field at the back. A firm called Chase had introduced glass cloches, a new idea. These consisted of four planes of glass kept together with wire clips to form a small greenhouse if placed end to end. They were about a foot high and 18 inches wide. We already had cold frames to use for protecting plants, but the advantage of the cloches was they could be picked up and carried around. They could be used for starting off the crop and then moved on to another once well established. We bought 300 yards of these and they were used on the nursery for over 50 years. I still have about 10 which I use in my garden now. I don't think plastic ones would have lasted quite as long.

The first new greenhouse we built was made by a firm with the name Skill. It was made of Dutch lights, a new idea from Holland. The lights, or frames, were made of a large piece of glass which slid into a frame of treated 1 ½" x 1 ½" wood. These frames were then fixed on to a steel structure. They were very quick to build and could even be moved if required. There was one big problem – they had clear glass doors and one night, just as it was getting dark, Fred walked through one of them thinking it was open. Luckily he didn't hurt himself. We soon boarded the doors up.

These houses had plenty of light and were good for growing salad crops. They did leak a little bit, where the Dutch lights butted together. Unlike the old houses, they didn't have to be painted, as they were pressure treated timber. Painting the greenhouses, which was done in the summer months, could be a very hot job sitting on the top of a greenhouse in the full heat of the day and the sun reflecting from the glass.

About half of the outside land, other than the paddock and the orchards, was still used for growing potatoes. Other crops were peas, broad beans, celery (which we had to dig trenches for), onions, shallots and green vegetables including Brussels sprouts. The worst winter jobs were picking Brussels on a cold frosty day and digging parsnips out of the frozen ground and then washing them in a large bath of cold water. We did grow a lot of runner beans in the summer months. They were the best paying of the crops. The best crop we ever had was the year they were grown on rotten silage which had come from the farm. This was in the early days of silage making. Apparently instead of the grass making silage it just turned rotten. To empty the silage pit the farm men were told they could dispose of it. The next few evenings and weekend they spent selling it round the village for £1 a load. We must have had about 12 loads. There was one problem – it still retained the smell of silage and it was quite a while before the village smelt sweet again.

To support the runner beans and peas we would pollard the lime trees which grew down the side of the nursery. The trees are still there now, but most of them have been allowed to grow very large. We also had a bed of rhubarb and this would have to be covered with straw in the late winter once it had a good frost on it. Some crowns would be lifted and put under the bench in the greenhouse to bring them on early.

We grew rows of tomatoes outside, starting them off with the cloches and then growing them up to four trusses. To ripen them in the autumn we took them off the bamboo supports, stripped the leaves and then laid them down in a row on straw, then covered them again with the cloches. Marrows would also be grown (courgettes had not become popular then). We were allowed to grow a few ridged cucumbers under the cloches.

A Growmore Club was formed for the local growers which covered most market gardens and nurseries in Hampshire. Meetings would be held on different holdings during the summer and in a hotel in Romsey during the winter, where ideas and advice would be exchanged. Dad was a very good tomato grower and as we sold all our crops retail in the shop he would only grow the variety Elsa Craig, a quality tomato. Most of the larger growers only grew the variety Potentate, a large cropper but very little flavour. I remember Dad saying at one of the meetings that because he grew for flavour he was able to get 6p a pound more for his tomatoes. He said the variety Potentate tasted more like a turnip than it did a tomato! Within a few years they were nearly all growing Elsa Craig.

All the work on the nursery was done by hand and one of the big winter jobs was what Grandad called "roughing up". This meant digging the soil over and leaving it rough in big lumps. He would say *"Don't pat it, it's not a dog"*. It was hard work with a five pronged fork. I always liked the look of it when it was finished and left for the rest of the winter. We liked to have the job done by Christmas so that the winter weather would break it down and leave a fine tilth for the spring. Another winter job was pruning and spraying the apples in the orchard. Pruning was a job I didn't like very much, it always seemed so cold and there was no way of keeping warm. Most of the apples we had were bush and had to be pruned keeping the centre open. I was told you should be able to sit in the middle of the tree and read a newspaper. Spraying with tar oil was a dirty job and hopeless if at all windy, when the spray would blow back in your face and sting. The only protection we had was an old mac and a hat and, if you were lucky, a pair of gloves. The smell of the tar stayed with you for weeks.

As time went by and food began to become a little more plentiful, restrictions on what we were allowed to grow were gradually eased and we were able to grow more flowers. Bulbs started to come in from Holland. Some of the bulbs were an enormous size, having been in the ground most of the war. One Carlton daffodil bulb produced 14 flowers. The azaleas and hydrangeas also started arriving from Belgium and had to be soaked in baths of water and potted up straight away. Three other flowering crops which we grew were chrysanthemums, carnations and violets. The carnations and chrysanths were mostly grown in large pots. The chrysanths were two or three plants to a pot and would be staked with a bamboo and stood outside during the summer. During hot weather they would need watering twice a day and in wet and windy weather they would always be blowing over. In September they would be moved into the greenhouses as the tomatoes were cleared. They would be all-bloom chrysanths, no spray, all different varieties flowering up to the end of November. There was really only one variety which would produce flowers naturally for Christmas. It was named "The Favourite" and had a rather shaggy white bloom. It also came in other colours such as yellow, pink and bronze. These would be grown in wire pots, plunged into the open ground in late May. They would be staked individually and tended during the summer. In September they would be lifted and brought into the greenhouse and planted in the borders. They would be flooded with water until they got established and with any luck they would flower at Christmas. Carnations would be grown one to a 10 inch pot, staked with bamboos and tied with raffia. They would have to be gone over about every six weeks. This entailed lifting each one on to an orange box, cleaning off any moss, tidying and tying up. I always felt this was a bit of a boring wet day job.

When working on the nursery we were able to tell the time by the buses going up the road. When we heard the 4.30 for Nether Wallop we knew it was only half an hour to tea time.

Dad grew a wonderful strain of Princess Elizabeth violets. They had large scented flowers on a long strong stem. Runners would be taken off the old plants when they had finished flowering in the spring and planted out in the nursery during the summer. Then in October they would be lifted on a spade and transferred into a cold greenhouse or frame, flower most of the winter and would be bunched in 12 blooms and a couple of leaves and tied with an elastic band. They always sold well. I remember the Rector, Rev. Thornby, often came in for them. On one occasion he asked me the name of a plant – it was Heliotrope, but I couldn't remember it. His reply was *"If you want to remember something, write it down, that's how I remember my sermon"*. He never used notes.

When the bulbs came in from Holland they would be either put in pots or in kipper boxes, which we obtained from the fishmongers. They were quite a bit larger than ordinary seed trays. All the daffodils and tulips would be grown for cut flowers. Some of the hyacinths would be grown to put in bowls for Christmas. Most of the flowers would be used in wreath work and bouquets.

One of the benefits of our job was that spring came a couple of months early. By the end of February we would put the heat up in one of the houses and start seed sowing and taking cuttings ready for the bedding season. John Innes potting compost was the only potting soil used at that time. John Innes compost was just a recommended formula which would be varied for different crops. This meant the main ingredient, which was soil, had to be sterilized to kill all the bugs and weed seed. In the days before this was done much time would be used later on weeding the trays and pots. We had a soil sterilizer, which was something like a copper on wheels. It had water in the bottom with sifted soil on top, kept above the water by metal grid with holes in it. The water was heated with a fire underneath, the steam then filtered up through the soil. The temperature had to be watched closely to make sure the soil didn't get overcooked. If this happened it would produce ammonia in the soil and would be no good for pricking out or sowing seedlings. The whole job was very labour intensive. The soil had to be shovelled in and out of the sterilizer and the whole job took a long time. Later on we had a much better method which consisted of a revolving drum with a flame thrower up the centre of the drum. It also had a sieve on the end which took out all the stones. This cut down the shovelling by quite a lot. Soil shovelling was a good job on a cold winter's day. Peat was also used; no more weeds from the leaf mould, and grit was preferred to silver sand in the mix. Like most nurserymen, we had our own preferred formula.

By the early 1950s things started to get a little easier. People became better off and there was more food and vegetables about. The interest in the flower garden began to return and with it came the demand for plants. Each year we increased the amount of bedding plants we grew. With the exception of geraniums and fuchsias, the bedding plants were all grown in seed trays, mostly 54 to a box. If a customer only wanted a dozen, they would be cut out of the boxes in a block and wrapped in newspaper, like fish and chips. The plants were much smaller than those sold today, which meant it took longer for them to mature. There was no instant garden in those days.

In the cold winter of 1947 I was playing football in a match on the rec. The pitch was frozen and slippery. I went over in a tackle and got kicked in the stomach. It was quite painful, but I carried on and it was not until the next day that I began to get a severe pain in my stomach. On the Monday I wasn't fit to go to work and Mum got the doctor, who sent me to hospital, where I remained for 10 days having x-rays and tests, which didn't really show anything. After about a week the pain began to disappear and they sent me home on 4th March, John's 21st birthday. Mum had me back at work the next day pricking out. She said I could sit down and do it. After that accident Dad said that if you wanted to work for yourself you couldn't really afford to have accidents playing football. As after this incident every time I played I got a headache I decided that it was time to give up football.

In 1947 we bought our first car, CPA 255, a Hillman. John learnt to drive with instructions from Mr. Moore of Ayling and Moore's garage. When they went out I sat in the back seat and listened. We had both applied for and got a provisional licence. There were no driving tests, it was possible to obtain a licence and then get into a car and drive it off. When John had learnt I got fed up with waiting for him to take me out, so I just got into the car and drove it to Crawley and back. In 1948 driving tests came in again. If you had held a provisional licence for over two years it wasn't necessary to take the test. As we had held ours for only a year we could still drive our car on our own, but we had to take the test within a year, which we did. We both passed first time.

Every morning the car was loaded with produce for the shop. This meant we no longer needed Horrie or Mr. Hillary. John would drive it in every morning except Friday, when I would do the trip. We also did any delivering there was to be done. I did this for a year or two, but I grew a bit fed up with it as I thought it was a bit of a waste of my time. I didn't fancy being a delivery boy. I also felt my time was better spent growing plants on the nursery.

When I was keeping my goats I had my milk round and Mr. and Mrs. Simpson were customers, who at that time lived in Fairclose Drive. They used to keep bees and sometimes when I called Mr. Simpson would say *"Come and have a look at the bees"*. He would take me to the hive, take the top off and blow cigarette smoke in to calm them. He invited me to have a look inside the hive to watch the bees working. I became very interested and when I left school decided to have a go at bee keeping. I wasn't short of help and advice from Mr. Saint and Mr. Cornelius, an old sailor who lived at The Haven who gave me a beehive and promised a swarm. One evening he arrived with a swarm of bees in an old-fashioned skip. I got a bit worried when he was walking with them through the orchard towards the hive over rather rough ground. He always walked as though he was still on board ship, but with luck he made it to the hive, where he shook them on to a white board in front of the hive. They then marched up into the hive as though they were animals entering the ark. A few weeks later Mr. Saint arrived with another swarm.

John Treadwell was the head of the bee-keeping department at the Farm Institute at Sparsholt and was taking evening classes on bee-keeping, so I decided to try and learn the job properly. The classes were held on winter evenings at Stockbridge School, which I attended. The following summer the bees produced my first honey crop and I sold most of it for half a crown a pound (12½p). The best result I ever had from one hive was when the field at the back of the nursery was sown with white clover. It produced 128 lbs of honey. One evening I was working on the hives when I looked up and who should be standing there but a well known actor, James Robertson Justice of "Doctor in the House" films. He was a customer of Dad's, who he liked to have a chat with. I was going to stop and serve him, but he said *"Carry on, I'm interested"*. I happened to move one of the hives and there was a slow-worm under it. Robertson Justice dived in, picked it up and gave it its correct Latin name and said *"My real job was an ornithologist, not an actor"*. At that time he lived at The Mill at Whitchurch and would often call in on his way to see his mother who lived at Twyford. He told Dad that if he was ever in Scotland to visit his house and garden on the west coast.

In 1947 the Winchester Horticultural Society revived their autumn chrysanthemum show in the Winchester Guildhall. I always enjoyed preparing and staging our trade stand. The show was held in November which was a quiet time in the nursery and it helped to brighten up a dull time of the year. I made the stand out of wood which screwed together. This was covered with a grey cloth which formed a lighter background for the flowers, rather than the black which was usually used for this purpose at that time. The exhibit was usually a mixture of flowers and floristry. For a few years we got the silver medal, but eventually we managed to get the coveted gold. It was an enjoyable event, meeting with old friends in the horticultural business. In the spring of 1948 the horticultural section of the National Farmers' Union held a market produce show on Southampton Common. The show covered all growers in Hampshire competing with each other in different classes. They were divided into small and large nurseries. We entered nine classes, winning three firsts, two seconds and three thirds. Getting first for a 12lb box of tomatoes gave me great satisfaction, having spent a long time sorting and polishing them. The prize Dad enjoyed most was beating Wills of Romsey, a very large nursery, with six hydrangeas in pots. They had six all pink, Dad had two pink, two blue and two red, which the judges seemed to think was more difficult to produce. We entered again the following year. We won a few prizes, but it was never quite the same again. The following year the show was extended to several other counties and moved to London.

Floristry was the best money-making part of the business, but I don't think Dad liked it as much as producing his beloved plants. When taking the orders for wreaths and bouquets it is very important to get the time right that they are required. Dad often told the joke against himself. He had been taking all the details from a young couple about the flowers for their wedding, when he inadvertently said *"What time is the funeral?"*. A lot of embarrassment all round! I gradually did more and more of the floristry work as I went along. It wasn't just wreaths; there would be cushions, hearts, gates ajar and all sorts of club badges, and for the gypsy funerals there would be horses and dogs and names. When I started making wedding bouquets they were made on what we called a drumstick, which was some moss bound with thin wire to a piece of bamboo, about ten inches long. The flowers would then be wired and the wire pushed into the moss. Sometimes roses were used, but mostly it would be carnations, made into a large bouquet with trailing fern nearly down to the ground. It made quite a heavy bouquet for the bride to carry. The design of brides' bouquets changed almost overnight after the Queen's wedding, when she carried a much smaller and lighter bouquet made with small flowers with the wires just bound together. It took a while to adapt, but once learned it was much easier. Out went the long trailing fern.

Making wedding bouquets was always more difficult than doing wreath work. The big problem was that it's the bride's one day in her life and we wanted to get it right. It was always easier if the bride knew exactly what she wanted, rather than the ones who didn't really mind and said they'd leave it to us. They were more likely to be the ones disappointed.

Two of our best customers were Sir Bernard and Lady Docker, who had a weekend house near Stockbridge called 'Sandydown'. They would come down from London for the weekend. Their butler, Mr. Jones, would ring up to order flowers to decorate the house, which was nearly always a van-load. Sir Bernard was chairman of several large national companies. Lady Docker was a noted character of the day and was often criticised in the papers for her lifestyle and her ability to upset people. Unknown to many, she did have another side. She befriended an old sailor who had lost both his legs and lived in an old people's home in Poole. I think he had written to her about her yacht 'Shamara'. She would collect him and take him out on the yacht. One day Mr. Jones, the butler, rang to order a wreath for £25. Dad said *"Do you mean 25 shillings?"*. That was about the usual price of a wreath at that time. He said *"No, £25."* It had to be taken to an undertaker in Poole. The old sailor had died and as he had no other relations it would be the only flowers at the funeral. As the funeral was early on a Monday, we had to work all day on Sunday making it and then deliver it. It was the largest wreath we had ever made. We had to make sure it wasn't too big to get into our shooting brake. We set out for Poole late on a very cold Sunday afternoon in February. It even looked as if it might snow. We took a shovel and a heater. Heaters were not fitted to cars at that time. We had a bit of a job finding the undertakers in Poole on a dark Sunday night, but eventually did so, before making for home cold and tired after a very unusual day.

Our customers, many of them regular, came from all walks of life. Many of the regulars became more like friends than customers. They ranged from Lords and Ladies, Judges, Archbishops and, of course, the average man in the street.

We sold to most of the churches in the district as well as the Cathedral. I got great satisfaction from going to the Cathedral at Christmas and seeing the large white chrysanthemums we had grown displayed on the altar. We also supplied hanging baskets, tubs and troughs to many of the pubs and shops in the district. For many years we supplied Mrs. Woodhouse at the Hampshire Chronicle office with the begonias, which always made a wonderful display over the old office front. In 1953, for the Coronation, we did several hundred baskets, all in red, white and blue. These included The Pentice in the High Street. It was quite rewarding to go round the town and district and see the plants we had grown flowering and giving colour and pleasure in many different locations.

On a summer afternoon in 1950, Michael, who had been our family dog for the past 16 years, passed away on the potting shed bench. We buried him under the trees at the bottom of the paddock with the rest of our family pets, including Daisy, my old goat. They all had a good life on the nursery.

By the early 50s, the number of people with cars increased and we started to get more customers coming on to the nursery. Quite a few of these were professional gardeners and Dad found it a big problem when they wanted to stop and talk. Some of them he encouraged to come in the evenings.

Business in the shop in Parchment Street gradually increased. Miss Portsmouth, when she became manageress of the shop, brought some of the customers from her father's old bakery shop with her.

By 1950 the number working on the nursery had increased to six.

Our England is a garden and such gardens are not made
By saying 'Oh how beautiful' and sitting in the shade
And when your back stops aching and your hands begin to harden
You will find yourself a partner In the glory of the garden
Rudyard Kipling

The Parchment Street shop opened by Grandad and Dad in 1926 now a clock shop

Nursery staff in the 1960s. John, John Perrin, myself, Anne, Dad and Peter Aylin

Grandad, Dad and Michael 'the half crown dog' and superb ratter outside the replacement greenhouse on the site of the original built in 1912

Most of the plants would have to be watered by hand

The 4.30p.m. King Alfred bus on its way to Nether Wallop. When we heard it go up through the village we knew it was only half an hour to 'knock off' time. If we were going to the pictures that evening we would catch it on its way back to Winchester at 6.00p.m.

The largest wreathe we ever made – ordered by Lady Docker to go to a funeral at Poole

Beekeeping – inspecting an empty hive

Wedding bouquets

Tape 8
Recreational Interests

My interests outside of working hours were quite diverse. Cricket came top of the list. I had been brought up in a family of cricket enthusiasts. Both Grandads and all the uncles and cousins played, or had played at some time. As small children John and myself would be taken to the Saturday match if Dad was playing. When quite young we would go down to the paddock with our bat, ball and stumps to play, sometimes in the evenings to be joined by Dad and Grandad. As we grew older we always looked forward to the start of the cricket season. Dave Weston, a bachelor who lodged with Mr. and Mrs. Gregory in Hollands Close, worked in the gardens at Lainston House and was the Littleton cricket club groundsman. He would get the old Atco mower out and start cutting the pitch and outfields. In the early days of the club in the 1920s Grandad had done this job with Joe and a horse mower. The cricket pavilion consisted of a First World War aeroplane packing case. It was about 12' long x 5' wide. It had a sort of veranda made of corrugated iron along one side, with two shutters underneath which lifted up so that it was possible to sit inside to watch the cricket or to score. I can still remember the wonderful smell of the pavilion. It was a mixture of grass, petrol given off by the mower, and linseed oil which was used on the cricket bats. At the start of the season it would be given a clear out and last year's kit would be sorted through. We boys would hang about in the hope that there might be an old broken bat which was no longer wanted. We would take it home, cut it down to size, bind it up and do any other repairs that may be required. Sometimes there might also have been an old ball with a broken seam, but was still good enough for us boys. On the Saturday afternoon of the first match we would get some old First World War wooden forms out and put them either side of the pavilion under the poplar trees. They disappeared many years ago. When the cricket started we would sit on the benches and watch. We would also put the numbers on the scoreboard when told to by the scorer.

After a while we would get a bit restless watching the cricket and start to wander off. We liked marvelling at Eddie Grace's motorbike, an Aerial. The speedometer went up to over 100 mph. Eddie at that time lived at South Wonston and was a keen member of the Littleton club. In later life he came and lived in the village.

The hedge on the other side of the ground was quite big and wide, much larger than it is now, and there was a cornfield on the other side. Sometimes the ball would be hit into the hedge or into the cornfield and a shout would go up *"Lost ball"*. Some of the men watching would try to find it. If they were unsuccessful the shout would then go up *"Penny on the ball"* and all the boys would tear off in the hope of finding it and claiming the reward of one penny, to spend on sweets in the village shop.

If Mum was helping with the teas, we would have tea with the men; cucumber sandwiches and dough cake, if I remember rightly. There would be a ladies versus men's match played in the evenings, when the WI would take on the men, who would have to play left handed and bowl underhand. Mum played tennis on the grass courts at the top of the rec. We would be ball boys and allowed to have a go ourselves now and again. There wasn't any football played before the war, mainly because there wasn't anywhere to make a pitch, as the ground above and below the cricket field was too rough and uneven.

Friday evening would be practice night, when the men would put up the nets. We would spend the evening fielding the ball for them. If we were lucky we would be allowed to have a go when they were finished. We had our heroes in the village team. There was Walt Brient who batted and bowled, and got 100 when playing against Flowerdown, which was a local derby and taken rather seriously. On one occasion when Littleton were playing Flowerdown another of our heroes, Rube Strong who lived on the Stud, Littleton's fast bowler, was bowling rather short pitched and hit the batsman in the ribs. The Flowerdown team had had enough and walked off, refusing to play. I think Rube must have been reading about the bodyline controversy in Australia. When he was trying to coach us boys, he used to say *"If you can't get them out, knock them out"*. That was about the limit of our coaching.

Another local derby match was against Sparsholt, the old enemy. As Mum's home was Sparsholt, we had divided loyalties in the family, Dad would be playing for Littleton and several uncles would be playing for Sparsholt. If Sparsholt happened to beat Littleton, Uncle Sid when he came on Monday with the bread, would pull Grandad's leg with some quip about Littleton being rabbits. Unfortunately Grandad didn't have a great sense of humour and it would be a few days before Grandad spoke to Uncle Sid again.

Quite a number of the older men would support the team and turn up to watch on a Saturday afternoon. Some would help with the umpiring and scoring. Mr. Ward, an old injured jockey who lived in Dean Down Drove, went to away matches in his pony and trap. He kept his pony on the old recreation ground on Flowerdown.

Grandad was passionately fond of cricket. He was a member of the Hampshire County Cricket Club. Once when he had been quite poorly, Mrs. Gill wrote to her husband who was working abroad, that when Mr. Hooker heard that England had beaten Australia in the Test Match, he was up digging the garden the next day.

The war brought an end to village cricket, but there were a few games played by the Home Guard. We boys would play among ourselves and when we got older became more organised and arranged matches with boys from other villages, like Kings Worthy and Hursley. We also played the students at the Farm Institute (now Sparsholt College). After the war it wasn't possible to play cricket at Littleton as football had taken over and was now being played across what was the cricket pitch. For this reason several of us who had been boys in the village before the war decided, after being invited, to go to Crawley to play cricket. They were John, his pal Alex, Reg Saint and myself. There would be matches Saturdays and Sundays, a new innovation, as cricket would not have been played on a Sunday pre-war. At Littleton there was a stipulation that no organised sport was to be played on the recreation ground before 12 o'clock on a Sunday, which we had to adhere to.

One of the problems at Crawley was that quite a number of the players were employed on the farm and could be called upon to work at a moment's notice, especially at haymaking and harvest. This meant we could be rung up and asked to play at short notice. The wickets were not very good then and sometimes you could find yourself playing the wicket more than the bowler. Many of the village wickets had been neglected during the war. Some villages used matting, which they would put down on the normal wicket. They did this at

Brown Candover. We would go to away matches in a small coach and very often call at the pub on the way home. Once, after playing at the Candovers, we stopped, I think it was at the Wheatsheaf, on our way home and Reg and myself had a glass of cider each. I was OK until I got home, when I began to feel rather ill, which lasted well into the night. When I met Reg the next day he said *"Gosh, I did feel bad when I got home last night"*. It was a long time before I drank cider again, in fact I still don't fancy it very much.

At the beginning of the 1953 season John, Alex and myself decided to leave Crawley and join the YMCA cricket team who were playing on their sports field at Weeke. Reg had given up cricket in favour of tennis. Our cousin, Bill Snow, had been the driving force in getting the team at Weeke under way a couple of years earlier and he encouraged us to join them. The following year Les Elms and Keith Guppy, who had been village lads, both joined as well, which meant nearly half the team originated from Littleton, and soon settled into a useful side. The ground was rather large and the pitch a bit slow, in spite of Bill's work on it. He put in many hours on the wicket. I can remember sometimes seeing him rolling it in the rain. The grass on the outfield was generally rather long, so a score of over 100 was quite reasonable. I remember one day seeing the ball hit for six clean over into the Stockbridge Road and going straight through the window of Ron Baton's garage, which was where Waitrose is now.

In the early 1950s the Tichborne Trophy was started. This was a 20-over competition played in the park between clubs in the Winchester district, played in the evenings on a knock-out principle. Two different teams every night, Monday to Thursday, gradually whittling the sides down until there were only two left, with the grand final in late July. The games drew a lot of interest and quite a large number of spectators and for the final they would be right round the ground. We always seemed to be drawn against St. Cross, who usually went on to win. It has taken county and national cricket over 50 years to realise that 20-over cricket is popular with spectators.

At that time John and myself were very keen on our cricket and we made a practice net with chicken wire in what was left of our old paddock and in the spring, as soon as the evenings got light enough about the end of February, we would have half an hour's cricket practice after work. John and myself usually opened the batting. Our aim was to get 30 on the board before the first wicket. At cricket we were opposites, John batted right and bowled left and I batted left and bowled right.

Unlike the cricket club in the village, tennis did manage to struggle on with just one court during the war. On the second court the grass was allowed to grow and after a while anthills appeared. Several of us boys became interested and started to play. There were the three Gill boys, two Phillips boys, Reg Saint and myself. We had to mow and mark the court before we could start playing. The mower was an old Atco which had been used pre-war to mow the cricket field and was nearly clapped out. It was a two-stroke engine, which was notorious for being difficult to start. It took us longer to get it going than to mow the court. At one time the clutch broke and we had to turn the handle to get it started and run along at the side at the same time. Once started you didn't dare stop until the court had been mown. The wire around the court was in a bad way with many holes. All it consisted of was wooden posts and chicken wire. The grass surrounding the courts was rough and long, so if the ball went over or through the wire, as it often did, there might be difficulty in finding it, which was rather important as balls were in short supply. We used them until they were bald and soft. When the war finished and the membership began to grow, the club became more organised. We brought the second court back into use. It was a difficult job getting it flat after the anthills and was rather rough for a couple of years. As we improved we started to play against other clubs, like Weeke and Crawley, who played on a court at the Dower House. I spent many happy hours in the summer on the courts playing tennis with my pals Alan, Eddie and Reg. On a Saturday I would play cricket in the afternoon and in the evening after the game I would spend the rest of the evening on the tennis court. I wish I had that amount of energy now!

Alan and myself would sometimes have a day at Wimbledon. It was in the days of Hoad and Rosewall. I remember standing in the corner on the Centre Court, a thing you could do in those days. Another thing we liked to do was have a trip to London. We would go up on the 9 o'clock train, wander round the shops in the morning and go to Leicester Square in the afternoon and watch the great Joe Davies play snooker. He always played with a handicap. We would have a meal at Lyons Corner House and then go on to a show. One show I remember seeing was 'Oklahoma' when it was first put on in Drury Lane. After the show we would tear downstairs out of the theatre to get across London to Waterloo in order to catch the last train home to Winchester. This was a real treat for us in the austere days of those times, although I don't think we realised how austere it really was as we couldn't remember anything different.

In 1947 the Rev. Thornley gave notice that he was going to hold confirmation classes. Alan, Eddie and myself, with others including several of the Denham family, joined the classes. My family had always been regular churchgoers, especially Granny and Grandad. I was introduced to Sunday school at an early age. It was held on Sunday afternoons. We would be divided up into age groups in different corners of the church. The oldest would be in the choir stalls with the rector. The teacher taking the youngest was Mrs. Dumper, who lived at Flowerdown bungalow. She didn't have any children of her own, but she was very kind to us little ones. Every time we attended we would be given a stamp with a biblical scene on it. This we had to stick into a book. We were told that if we wanted to go on the Sunday school outing we had to have so many stamps in the book. I think this may have been just a bribe to encourage us to go to Sunday school. I can't recall anyone being barred. The outing was nearly always to Hayling Island. There was great excitement waiting for the King Alfred coach to arrive. They were much smarter than the old buses which took us to school. The wooden bridge into Hayling was quite old and had not been built to take the weight of a coach with 40 children on board. When we arrived at the bridge we would have to disembark, walk over the bridge and get back on board the coach on the other side. The main attraction to us boys was the funfair, especially the lake with the island in the middle inhabited by monkeys. It wasn't so much the monkeys that attracted us, but the small motorboats for hire. I went with John in one and when our time was up John drove the boat to the far side of the lake and tried to hide as much as he could behind the island in the middle, hoping the boat attendant wouldn't see us.

In 1937 we joined the church choir. Mr. Hinxman was the organist and choirmaster. The choir was mixed and the girls sat one side, mainly the Denham girls, and the boys the other. The services alternated, morning service one week, evensong the next. We had to be careful to behave during the sermon as the rector's housekeeper would sit in the second row from the front and keep an eye on us, so you had to be careful if you happened to flick a piece of sweet-paper at the girls on the other side. We would have choir practice on Friday nights and in the winter would have to walk home in the dark. Like most young boys we did our best to frighten the girls. One night I shouted *"Look out!"* and they all ran down the village screaming. The following week Mr. Hinxman walked home with us, pushing his bike. We would be paid one penny for the practice and one for the service, and be paid half a crown for weddings and funerals. The organ was quite old and in a rather poor state, which I understand made it difficult to play. It still had to be pumped by hand. One of the choirboys would have to do it if the regular pumper was away. This required a reliable boy as it relied on concentration to keep sufficient air in the organ. There was a lead weight on a piece of string which went up and down according to the amount of air. The art was to keep the organ with the maximum amount of air by gently pushing the handle up and down. The amount of air needed depended on the music being played. Sometimes if there was a loud piece of music and the pumper wasn't concentrating and he suddenly realised the lead weight showed nearly empty, there would be the sound of frantic pumping which could be heard in the church. The organist and the rector would not be very pleased. Because he was reliable, John had the job of pumping the organ for many years.

Because of ill health Mr. Hinxman had to give up being organist and choirmaster and as there was no permanent organist the choir began to dwindle and we lost interest. Early in the war, however, we did get a new choirmaster, Mr. Bradbury. He was a teacher from Portsmouth Grammar School who had been evacuated to Winchester. He brought some boys from the school with him and, not to be outdone by boys from Portsmouth, several village boys re-joined, which made it an all boys choir.

The Rev. Thornley was quite elderly when he took on the job of rector of Crawley and Littleton. All he appeared to do was to take the Sunday services together with funerals and weddings. He lived in the Rectory at Crawley and never did much parish visiting. He did come into the nursery sometimes to buy flowers and if you hadn't been to church for a while he would say *"I haven't seen you in church lately"*. He must have been well into his 70s and as he got older the church congregation began to dwindle. The services would change to matins at Crawley and evensong at Littleton. It was quite sad because in his younger days he had been active. He became rather unpopular in the village and when the two boys were killed at Farley Mount the parents didn't want him to take the funeral service. They asked for the Rev. Tanner, a schoolmaster who lived in Weymouth and had been chairman of the building of the village Memorial Hall and still spent the school holidays with his mother who lived at St. Swithun's, the white house in the village. He would help the Rev. Thornley on special occasions, like Easter, harvest and Christmas, which we choirboys were always pleased about. After the service we would be invited to his mother's house and given apples and cakes. Grandad was a great friend of the Rev. Tanner and gave strict instructions that he was to bury him and not the Rev. Thornley. It was mainly the hard work of Mr. Denham, the churchwarden, which kept the church going. Granny and Grandad went to evensong as long as they could. They always walked, no matter what the weather. I remember Granny coming into church on a very wet and windy night and the rector saying *"Brave woman"*. The Rev. Thornley did take us for confirmation instruction on Sunday afternoons and on a sunny March Sunday in 1945 Alan, Eddie and myself, and several other teenagers from the village, together with our parents, were conveyed on one of the small Dennis King Alfred buses to St. Cross, where we were confirmed by the Bishop. When the British Legion paraded to church on Armistice Sunday we boys, who were members of the boys club, would march behind. When we arrived at the church the rector would ask what evenings the club met and would say *"I must come one evening",* but he never did.

After I had given up playing football I still liked to support the boys' team and sometimes be linesman. Several of the village men, including Dad, also liked watching the game. On one occasion I was running the line and signalled the ball had gone over. Dad shouted out *"No it hasn't"*. With that, the ref. blew his whistle and, among much hilarity amongst the men, proceeded to tell Dad off, saying *"Leave the boy alone, he knows what he's doing"*. The ref. did see the funny side of it after the game when he was told we were father and son and that it was part of Dad's sense of humour. My cousin Gerald was a very good footballer and was picked when he was 16, 17 and 18 to play for the Hampshire National Association of Boys' Clubs. They were a very good team and travelled far and wide to play. Sometimes we would have a small coach to go and watch them. I think it was some of the best football I ever saw. It was good, clean, pure football.

One good piece of advice I have remembered all my sporting life was given to me by an old village character, George Gregory. We were watching the Littleton boys playing the Stanmore boys. They were always a thorn in our side. We seldom beat them and I said to him *"We shall never beat them, look how big Stanmore is compared to Littleton, they have so many to pick from"*. He looked at me and said *"Ah, but they've only got 11 in the team the same as you"*. I've always remembered that when playing teams supposed to be superior to us.

On Easter Monday the Hampshire National Association of Boys' Clubs held their annual six a side tournament made up of boys' clubs from all over Hampshire at the Sports Centre in Southampton. One year amongst great excitement we managed to win it, beating a team from Eastney in Portsmouth in the final. For a village to do it was a bit like David and Goliath.

When many of the lads became too old to play in the boys' team they formed an adults' side and as several of them came from Sparsholt they decided to call themselves Sparton, a combination of the names Sparsholt and Littleton. They carried on for a number of years, but finally finished in the late 50s.

Another occasion I remember at that time was the Queen's wedding. We listened to the radio most of the day and in the late afternoon we went into Winchester to see them as they were to arrive at the station on their way to Broadlands in Romsey for their honeymoon. We watched them from Station Hill get into the car and drive down the hill. We then ran up Station Path and across the bottom of the Arbour and saw them again drive up the Romsey Road. The wedding had been a glimmer of light amongst the austerity of those times and patriotism was still something to be proud of.

The farmer and the gardener
are both at church again.
The one to pray for sunshine,
the one to pray for rain.
Tracey Bovey

Littleton cricket club 1930. Back row from left: Grandad, Dave Weston, Ted Reading, Len Smith, Norman Goater (uncle), Reg Guppy, Fred Hooker (uncle). Front row from left: S Jarvis, Harold Goater (uncle), Dad, George Gregory, Tom Maggs

YMCA cricket team. Back row from left: M Wright, J Marshall, G Strange, J Rickman, P Beckwith, L Elms, G Smerdon, P Eldridge. Front row from left: J Hooker, B Snow, A Smith. Major General Pratt, myself, W Alexander, D Walker, C Emery

On the old grass courts. Alan Gill, Connie and myself taking a rest between sets sitting on the old roller

1947 Boys Club 18 and under team playing in the final of the Colebrook cup Littleton lost to Stanmore after a replay. I had just come out of hospital and was unable to play back row from left: Myself, A Ware, G Barret, K Guppy, C Ketley, E Thompson, M Goater, E Newman. Front row from left: N Smart, G Goater, P Elms, a n other, a n other.

Tape 9
Winchester Operatic Society

In May of 1946 I went to the Guildhall to see the Winchester Operatic Society which was just re-forming after the War. They were performing a concert version of Edward German's Merry England. I had been encouraged to do so by Clarice Portsmouth when I had been in the shop. The leading soprano soloist was Vera Portsmouth, who I had met in several walks of life, from school, to boys' club, to tennis. I was very impressed by the high standard of the singers and chorus and really enjoyed the evening. In September the same year there was an advert in the Hampshire Chronicle for members for Iolanthe, the opera to be performed the following spring. A date for auditions, which were to be held at Stanmore, was given. I remember seeing it, but gave it no further thought.

About a week after the auditions I happened to be in the shop again and Clarice asked me if I'd thought of joining the Operatic Society. To this I replied that I hadn't really because I didn't have much experience of singing and I didn't think I had a voice good enough. She said they were very short of men and as long as you could stand up, you would be in! The first rehearsal was to be that evening and there would be auditions beforehand. She also tried to get John to join. I said that I would think about it back at home on the nursery. I talked it over with John. He said he definitely wouldn't have a go. After a lot of thought I decided I would give it a try. Little did I realise at the time that it would be a decision that would have a considerable effect on the rest of my life. I contacted Clarice and told her my decision, but that John wouldn't be joining. That evening I set off on my bike for Stanmore School, which was familiar to me because I remembered it from schooldays. I made my way to the hall where the Committee were holding auditions. Jack Sealey, the Musical Director, asked me for my song, to which I replied that I didn't know that I had to bring one. They said *"you had better sing some scales"*, which I did. After a short deliberation they decided that they would put me on reserve as a bass, which would be reviewed at Christmas. For the rehearsal that followed we assembled in the main school hall and were divided up into sopranos in the front on the left, with the altos on the right, and at the back the tenors were on the left with the basses on the right. I joined the basses with Roy Portsmouth, Clarice's brother and Vera's husband. He was about the only man who I really knew. I shared his score, which I didn't really understand, not being able to read music. Being a choirboy I had only sung the topline, or the melody. The rehearsal was to be what Mr. Seeley called "a run through". He raised his baton, the accompanist Mrs. Saunders, started to play and he brought the chorus in and away we went. I remember my surprise at the wonderful sound. I soon got the idea that the basses were singing their own line, although I wasn't able to contribute much on that first evening.

The next day I went into Whitwams music shop and bought a score. They were only half the size of a normal score because of the paper shortage. When I got home I put it on the piano and started playing with one finger the bass part. I found this a great help at rehearsal the following week. Rehearsals were every Wednesday evening and after a few weeks I felt I was really getting into it. I did feel a little isolated, not knowing many people. There was very little time to meet in the interval and I was still not a very confident young man. I felt much happier at the social evening, which was held in November. At Christmas the names of those who were to play the principal parts were announced and I was told by the Chairman that I was to be taken off the reserve and made a full member of the chorus. By Christmas we had to know all the chorus words and music by heart. In the New Year the chairs were cleared away and we started to learn the stage positions and moves; shortest at the front and tallest at the back. The best part for the men is the entrance of the Peers' chorus. The chorus and principals would rehearse every Wednesday evening and the principals alone would have to rehearse on the Thursday. By the end of March we rehearsed both evenings. As the show became nearer rehearsals became more intense. Most members would travel to rehearsals by bus or, like me, by bike. Very few cars were used as petrol was still in short supply. The Producer came from Southampton by bus and the Conductor came on his bike.

About three weeks before the show the box office opened at Whitwams and on the first morning there would be a queue for tickets, mostly for the last night. On Sunday afternoon, 9th May 1948, we arrived at the Winchester

Guildhall to try on our costumes, which we had been measured for about six weeks before. Our dressing room was a rather drab room at the back of the Guildhall. It wasn't very large and smelt damp, but we had plenty of costumes to put on, with coronets either over your eyes or sitting on the top of your head like a pea on a drum! We also had to rehearse entrances and exits, which wasn't easy with a large cast and very little room at the sides and back of the stage. We spent the whole of Monday evening rehearsing on the stage, learning how to cope with a cast of 48 on quite a small stage. On the Tuesday evening, to be ready for the curtain up at the dress rehearsal, we were asked to arrive at the Guildhall as early as possible for make-up, as this took a long time. Some members who could would arrive as early as 5 o'clock. Once made up we would sit in the green room, the banqueting hall, and chat. For the first time we had an orchestra of 28. It took a while to get used to it after just having a piano. Some of the senior citizens of the town were invited, so it meant that we had an audience for the first time. All the rehearsing paid off and as the week went on we were able to relax a little and enjoy ourselves. On the Saturday there were two shows, a matinee in the afternoon, with tea in the banqueting hall between the shows. After the show on the last night there was a parade of stewards up the middle of the hall, each holding a bouquet in his hands. These were presented to the lady principal and cast. We then all went into the banqueting hall to meet our friends and relations. I remember Mum being quite excited about the whole thing and me being involved. When the show was over we all felt a little bit like a deflated balloon. We had spent the last eight months rehearsing and the last week we had spent a large amount of our time at the Guildhall, some nights nearly until midnight. We had become a bit like a large family, working together to produce the show.

    I felt I had been very fortunate to be part of a society with a tradition of producing shows of a very high standard, the first of which was Pirates of Penzance performed in 1913. I believe the idea had originated from members of the Cathedral choir, among the names I seem to remember were Mr. Whitwam, Mr. Masters, and one I really do remember, Archie Clements, a wonderful old Winchester character. The following year they produced the Mikado. Because of the First World War it was not until 1920 that they performed Iolanthe. They then performed shows every year until 1939, just before the Second World War. During that time they had several well known conductors; Sir Malcolm Sergeant,

Sir Dan Godfrey and Muir Mathieson. One of the main producers was Noel Hanbury, who lived at The Grange at St. Cross. They were the people who set the standard which the Society now had to endeavour to live up to.

On the Monday evening after the show a dinner dance was held in the Guildhall. This brought the season to a close. For me it had been a wonderful experience being part of it. Although it had been difficult to begin with, as the season went on I enjoyed it more. I didn't miss a single rehearsal and I had difficulty in believing that I had been part of something like this. I made up my mind to have a go again if possible the following year.

The show for 1949 was to be the Gondoliers and in early September a record evening was held, when the music of the Gondoliers was played through, with the producer giving a short talk about the show. The auditions were to be held towards the end of the month, so if I wanted to join I had to find a song to sing. I looked through some of Dad's old songs and the only one I found which seemed suitable was Drake Goes West. I practiced it with the help of one finger on the piano and eventually got Dad to accompany me on the piano. I went to the audition feeling very nervous, but I somehow managed to get through it. Unlike the previous year, there were more men auditioning than required and I wasn't very confident of even getting on the reserve. The results were posted to us and I opened the envelope with considerable apprehension, but much to my surprise I had been accepted as a full member. I had a job to believe it. The Gondoliers was great fun, especially for the chorus. It kept us busy as some of us had three or four changes of costume. I encouraged my friend Reg Saint to join and help back stage, where he met his future wife, Marion, who lived at Littleton. She was also in the chorus. The show was again a great success with a full house most nights. The opera fitted in well with my social life. It meant I could spend the winter rehearsing the opera and the summer playing cricket and tennis.

The show for 1950 was to be Patience, but at the AGM there was a certain amount of disagreement, as it was felt that the Society didn't have a person suitable to play the part of Bunthorne. However, they needn't have worried as a new Cathedral chorister joined, Bertram Dobson, who was a tenor and also a very good actor. We had to go through the process of auditioning every year. I again sang Drake Goes West and was accepted for the chorus. After the auditions for principal parts, which were held in November, it was always interesting to hear the new principals singing at the rehearsals. This year it was Mr. Dobson, who had a lovely tenor voice. When the person who was to play Patience sang she had this lovely soprano voice. It was Connie Smithers, who had been in the chorus for the last couple of years. We had been at Stanmore School together, but she was a year ahead of me and we didn't have a lot of contact. She was very slim and slight and it was amazing where this lovely soft but strong voice came from. After the principal parts were announced in November, much to my amazement I was asked by the committee if I would like to understudy the small part of the Major. I hadn't even thought of auditioning, but after I had recovered from the shock I said I would have a go. This meant I had to attend principal rehearsals on Thursday evenings. The part of the Major was being taken by Peter Chew who, with his wife, had been a dancing instructor back in the boys' club days. One evening at rehearsals Peter told me he wouldn't be able to attend the next principal rehearsal and would I be prepared to stand in for him. I swatted up the part with the help of the old 78 record I had. Much to my relief I quite enjoyed the rehearsal with help from Mervyn Hayne and Bruce Taylor, who were playing the other two military men. At the end of the rehearsal Bertram Dobson said *"You've got a nice voice, why don't you have singing lessons?"*. I think my reply was that I didn't think it was that good, and left it at that.

The following day Mum had been in the shop in town and had met Mr. Dobson, who told her that I should have my voice trained and she had fixed up for me to have singing lessons with a Madam Shearer who lived in Bournemouth and came up to Winchester to give lessons one day a week at Whitwams in their shop in the High Street. I fixed a time for an audition with her and when I arrived there was this rather stout, round lady in her 60s I suppose. I think I sang a verse from a song. She said *"Mr. Dobson knows what I like"* and that she would be only too pleased to take me on as a singing pupil. Her main instruction would be on voice production. I fixed up a time which had to be after I'd finished work at 5 o'clock. Having singing lessons was another of those things which altered my life. It helped me by giving me more confidence. She was a very confident lady and she helped pass that confidence on to her pupils. I was having a lesson one day and I said to her *"The great Peter Dawson doesn't do it like that"*. She looked at me and said *"You're not Peter Dawson, you're Austen Hooker. You do it the way it suits you. Be yourself."* She also had a sense of humour. When I started going to lessons in the car instead of on my bike, I would be her last pupil of the day and I would give her a lift to the station to catch her train back to Bournemouth, which she always left to the last minute. Very often the train would be pulling into the station as we went up Station Hill. When we were leaving Whitwams we had to come out of the side passage as the shop had been shut some time before. As she was a rather round lady she found this rather difficult, as there were often musical instruments stored there, and as we squeezed out through them she would say *"Turn sideways madam, but what do you do if you don't have a sideways!"*. I enjoyed my singing lessons with my Diack book of singing exercises. She was also a great believer in oratorio for training, especially Elijah for bass baritone, which she claimed I was. She was a great believer in getting the vowels right. This I found difficult with my broad Hampshire accent. She was also not keen on my trying for principal parts in the opera for a couple of years until I was producing my voice correctly.

The rehearsals for Patience were changed from Stanmore School to a small hall which was at the junction of Romsey Road and West End Terrace, which I believe belonged to St. Thomas' Church. This was rather small and a bit run down. When the chorus of Dragoon Guards were doing their sword drill, one of the men put his sword down with such a thump it went clean through the floor. Most of the members would either ride their bikes or walk to rehearsals, but after rehearsal would divide up into groups to make their way home. I very often joined the group who were making their way towards Fulflood and Weeke and although I had my bike I would very often walk with them, as several of them were friends. Some I remember were Ray, Mac, Stella and Connie, who was playing Patience. On principal rehearsal nights there was only Connie and myself making our way in that direction and as it was a rather dark walk under the beech trees near the prison wall I asked her if she would like me to accompany her as far as her home in Western Road. In conversation she said she enjoyed playing tennis, so I said to her *"Why don't you come and join us at Littleton next summer?"*. Although not one of the more popular Gilbert and Sullivan shows, Patience was performed the following spring, with great success.

After it was all over Connie and a friend from the opera, Mac, joined us at the club at Littleton. Mac had an old Morris car which they came out in. Sometimes Connie would ride her bike. They both joined in the playing in the matches with other clubs. Mac was a very good player, but when we played in matches Mac was very nervous and her game would sometimes go to pieces. On one occasion four of us from the club went to London in Mac's car, Connie, Mac, Alan and myself. It was a bit of a hair raising journey as Mac was a bit of an erratic driver. We went to see the D'Oyly Carte Pirates of Penzance at the Sadlers Wells Theatre, as this was to be the Winchester show for 1951.

The opera at the Guildhall in May was a popular event in the City, but 1951 was to be Festival of Britain year and this year's opera was to be an extra special event. We were to perform two operas, Trial by Jury followed by the Pirates of Penzance, with an extra performance on the Friday night of the previous week of the show. It was to be a Civic Night, held in conjunction with the City Mayor. Among those who attended were members of the City Council, County Mayors and Mayoresses and members of the Consular Corps and their wives. This meant we were now doing 12 performances over 10 days and were at the Guildhall for two weeks, which included rehearsals and dress rehearsals. It was quite hard going doing a day's work and then performing in the evening, but we were young and enjoyed every minute of it. I was again lucky and was picked to play a member of the jury in Trial, and a pirate in the first act and a policeman in the second act in Pirates. Connie was a bridesmaid in Trial and one of General Stanley's daughters in Pirates.

During the following summer I went with Connie to the Festival of Britain. It is a job to remember now what our feelings were at the time, it was so different to any previous experience. For the first time since we were children we were looking forward, with the years of austerity behind us. Later in the day we had a trip on a boat down the Thames to the Battersea Funfair, which was part of the Festival.

The opera for 1952 was to be Princess Ida, one of the lesser known Gilbert and Sullivan operas, which called for a rather large cast of principals. With Madam Shearer's approval I auditioned for a minor part and was successful in being given the part of Guron, one of King Gamas's three sons. It didn't call for any solo singing, just part of a trio. The other two sons were played by Cecil Sacree and Rob Wilton. We became friends, spending a lot of time rehearsing together. Rob sang all the solo parts, he had a really wonderful bass voice and we became really great friends for the rest of his life.

At Christmas 1951 Connie and myself became engaged, with the task now to find somewhere to live. We also had to decide where would we be married.

Connie always attended her parish church of St. Paul's where, during the war years she had been instructed for confirmation by a young go-ahead curate, the Rev. H. C. N. Williams. He had returned to Winchester recently as rector of St Bartholomew's Hyde, where he created a very thriving community. As the church in Littleton had become very low, we decided to attend Hyde, where we were made very welcome and after a time were put on the electoral roll. I never fell out with the church in Littleton, it was just that the Rev. Thorney was rather old and we were young. I must say that when I eventually asked him to call my marriage banns he said *"Austen, nothing would give me greater pleasure."* I think they must have been the last banns he called, by the time we were married he had retired. We were in the same position as many young people are today, trying to find somewhere to live that we could afford. Some things never change. I was offered a bungalow in Fairclose Drive for £3,000, but I couldn't afford the mortgage. I had £500 in my savings so we decided to try to get planning permission to put a caravan on the nursery. I eventually got permission, but I had to re-apply every year. We spent several weekends looking at caravans and eventually found what we wanted at the Redskin Caravan Co. at Chichester. I levelled a site near the back of the bungalow so that I could run electricity across. It arrived on Good Friday 1953 and after much shunting around we got it into position. I connected the electricity and got cold water laid on.

When fixing the date for the wedding we had a problem. The opera, the Mikado, was fixed for the third weekend in May and we both had principal parts. Connie was to play Yum Yum, one of the three little maids, and I was to play Pish Tush, my first solo principal part. We fixed the date for the wedding for Saturday, 25th April, three weeks before the show. This made life a bit hectic, attending rehearsals and preparing for the wedding. When asked if we would like the choir, we said we would bring our own, the Operatic Society.

It was very much an operatic wedding, with Connie being given away by Stanley Richardson, her boss at Richardson and Starling, who was also playing Ko-Ko in the Mikado. My sister Anne and Connie's friend, Margaret Bone, were bridesmaids. Connie carried a small bouquet, no long trailing fern, which I made with pink Madame Butterfly roses grown by our friends Mr. and Mrs. Moore at their Sutton Scotney nursery. Anne and Margaret carried bouquets of pink carnations. John was my best man, with Bill Snow and Alan Gill as stewards. The reception was held in Hyde Parish Hall. Aunty Elsie from Sparsholt had made the cake. This wasn't easy at that time as rationing of some things was still in existence. As Grandad wasn't very well, after the reception John took Connie and myself out to Littleton to see both Granny and Grandad before we went back to Connie's to change. We spent our honeymoon at Bournemouth. This could only be for three days, as we had to be back by the Wednesday evening for the Mikado rehearsal.

At that time the National Hard Court Championships were held at Dean Park, Bournemouth, so we spent one day there, but it was rather cold. The weather the week before had been warm and sunny, but it changed cold on the Saturday. The photo's I have while we were away show me with my overcoat on.

On the Wednesday we returned to Littleton to our new home in the caravan and that evening we went to the opera rehearsal.

The flowers that bloom in the spring
Tra La,
Breathe promise of merry sunshine
As we merrily dance and we sing
Tra La,
We welcome the hope that they bring
Tra La,
Of a summer of roses and wine.

From the Mikado by Gilbert and Sullivan

Happy times with the Winchester operatic society. A peer in Iolanthe – my first show

Programme

Clarice Portsmouth, myself and Marion Watts – we all lived in Littleton

Connie's first principal part as Patience

Myself as the usher in Trial by Jury – Mum did not like me made up to look so old but I always enjoyed playing this part

Three Little Maids – the Mikado 1953
L-R: Anne Hillier, Connie, Hazel Ponsford

I'm on the right on stage with two of the greats of the society in H.M.S. Pinafore – Horace Taylor, Bertram Dobson

Our wedding at St Bartholomew's Church, Hyde on 25 April 1953

Tape 10
Early Married Life

The Hampshire Chronicle report of our wedding was headed "Pish Tush marries Yum Yum", the characters we were playing in The Mikado, which turned out to be a tremendous success, with a full house nearly every night. Altogether about 3,000 people saw the show. Being in the Operatic Society brought me back into contact with my old headmaster from Peter Symonds, Dr. Freeman. He was a very keen Gilbert and Sullivan fan and was Vice President of the Society. I remember one evening when we were rehearsing at the Guildhall, he was sitting with Archie Clements, a past Principal, when they beckoned me over and gave me some very good advice, which was that when you are talking to someone on the stage, remember you are actually speaking to the person in the back row of the gallery. The only time I was performing on stage with Connie was the madrigal in the second act. Connie's doctor, Ronald Gibson, was also a Vice President and later became President. He also became Sir Ronald Gibson, for the work he did as Chairman of the BMA.

As it was Coronation year, The Mikado was part of Winchester's celebration. The list of dignitaries on the civic night was as long as your arm. They included the Duke of Wellington; the Lord Chancellor Lord Symonds, who lived at Sparsholt; the General Administrator of the D'Oyly Carte Opera Company; the High Sheriff of Hampshire; some of the Consular Corps from Southampton; and most of the Mayors of Hampshire and many others. This time must have been the heyday of the Operatic. The war had been over for just long enough for people to start feeling they could afford to go out to shows and, of course, TV was still a luxury and only in a few homes. When I look back on it now I find it hard to believe that we were part of it. It seems rather like a dream.

Connie had been singing at concerts and functions for a number of years. The first concert I sang solo at was held by the WI in the village hall. I remember I was rather nervous singing in front of many people who I knew and messed up my words in one song. Something I never did in all the years I was in the Operatic. I said that in future I would take my words with me, but Connie talked me out of it because she felt that once you started doing that you would always want to take them. We also started singing together at different functions, finishing up with a couple of duets.

Like many people, Mum and Dad bought a television especially to watch the Coronation. On the morning of the great day about eight of us gathered round the television to watch the service in Westminster Abbey and the procession through London. In the afternoon the village celebrations started with a carnival procession through the village, starting at the top of the hill at the end of Dean Down Drove. Most of the village children wore fancy dress. The procession was led by the WI dressed in costumes of the Court of Elizabeth the First, Mrs Davis was dressed as Elizabeth the First. The music for the procession was provided by Brigham Young with a record player carried in the back of our shooting brake, with myself, dressed as a Dragoon Guard, sat on the roof holding the loudspeaker.

At about 5 o'clock Connie and myself made our way into Winchester to be on the float of the Operatic Society, which was to take part in the carnival procession through Winchester. The float was one of Horace Taylor's lorries decorated with several scenes from Gilbert and Sullivan operas. Members were dressed in costumes from the different operas. Connie wore the costume of one of the three little maids from the Mikado, I wore the uniform of a Dragoon Guard from Patience. Anyone who remembers Coronation Day knows how cold and damp it was for June. Some of the girls on the float wore flimsy costumes and they felt rather cold. The six of us who were dressed as Guards were lucky, we had to walk by the side of the float and were able to keep reasonably warm. There were a lot of floats all depicting the many interests and aspects of life in the city. When we arrived back in Littleton the celebrations were still going on. There had been sports and a tea party for the children in the afternoon and a whist drive for the adults. We arrived back just in time for the social and dance, which went on until midnight.

About a fortnight later a coach trip was arranged to go up to London to see the decorations and lights. The coach left Littleton at about 6. 00 p. m. picking up people on the way. When we arrived it was still light and we divided up into groups and wandered round, gazing at the wonderful decorations and, when it became dark, the lights. It was a lovely, warm summer night. I don't suppose today it would have the same impact, but we were still recovering from the effects of the war and years of austerity. When we arrived back home it was just getting light. We only had a couple of hours sleep and were back at work in the morning.

I must have been one of the few newly married men whose wife was a better cook than their mother. Like everything Connie does, she does well and her cooking is no exception. I don't mean Mum was a bad cook, but I think she had learnt all her cooking in the bake house at Sparsholt on a large scale, but she kept us well fed during the war years, making a little go a long way.

We were now settling in to living in the caravan and for the two of us it was really cosy. When the bed was up in the wall and the table put up we had a dining area near the kitchen and a lounge area at the opposite end. As Granny didn't make a cup of tea after dinner at mid-day and Grandad was now well enough, he would walk down the nursery and call in on us every day at about 1.30 for his cup of tea. One thing living in a caravan taught me was that you have to be tidy and put things in their proper place.

We often think in life that it's a good thing we don't know what's round the corner. One Sunday in July I didn't know that it was going to be one of the most difficult days of my life. There was a village outing to the Isle of Wight and Mum and Dad and Anne and Richard went with most of the village. John was away and I was left to look after the nursery. The weather was quite warm, so there was plenty of watering to do in the morning and when I had finished I looked in on Granny and Grandad to see if they were OK. Grandad said that he was going on the bus to watch the cricket at Crawley in the afternoon. We had our Sunday lunch and were sitting down in the caravan when we saw Granny coming round the corner looking very worried. She said that Grandad had collapsed in the toilet and she couldn't open the door. Apparently he had gone out to catch the bus to Crawley, but came back to the toilet. I ran up to the house and tried to push the door back, but couldn't hold it back long enough to get in. I was in a quandary as to where to get help as so many in the village were on the outing. I remembered Brian Gill from next door hadn't gone and I was able to get him to help me. We were able to push the door enough for me to squeeze in, lift Grandad up and get the door open. We put him in a wheelchair and got him on the bed. By this time Granny and Connie had arrived. How Granny had managed to walk down to us and back we never knew, as she had not been able to walk very far for several years. I think Connie must have rung for the doctor and Aunt Flo. Granny said *"get Miss Wort"*, a retired nurse who lived over the road at The Hollies. When she arrived she said Grandad was, as we suspected, dead. This was confirmed by the doctor when he arrived. I then had to do what was one of the most difficult jobs of my life. Miss Wort had to lay him out, but she was rather frail and unable to lift him. Granny and Aunt Flo, who had arrived by this time, asked me to help her. I thought afterwards that it's amazing what you can do when you have no choice. Another difficult task was to meet the coach and tell Dad when he arrived back from the outing. Needless to say, he was very upset. As was the custom in those times, Grandad was laid out in his coffin in the front room. People would call and pay their respects. I couldn't see him like that, I just wanted to remember him as I knew him on the nursery.

When I look back I realise how very fond of him I was and what great admiration I had for him for what he had done with his life, which started as a twelve year old ploughboy on a farm. I realise that so many of the things he enjoyed and the interests he had he passed on to us boys. He always enjoyed taking an active part in the community, especially in the village which he helped to establish in those early years of development. He was a member of the first Parish Council, the first Cricket Club and the village Flower Show. He negotiated on behalf of the Council the purchase of the recreation ground, he was the Secretary of the Hall Committee, building the village hall. He was also a founder member of the British Legion and a loyal member of St. Catherine's Church, where his funeral took place. He requested that the Rev. Tanner should take the service. The church was full, reflecting the many interests of his life, with Lieutenant Colonels mingling with the gardeners. The coffin was draped with the Union Jack and a guard of honour was formed by the British Legion and the South African War Veterans' Association with their standard. After the service he was laid to rest in the tranquil beauty of the little village cemetery. Granny was not well enough to attend the funeral, but she decided to carry on living in the old house on her own.

Holidays that summer consisted of days out in the car. Mum, Dad and Richard usually came with us to places like Lepe, New Milton and Highcliffe. The autumn brought the cricket season to an end and the start of rehearsals for the opera, which was 'Ruddigore', one of the lesser known Gilbert and Sullivan operas. We were able to go to the Kings Theatre, Portsmouth, to see it performed by the D'oyly Carte Opera Company. On the way home the coach stopped on the top of Portsdown Hill, where we had a late picnic admiring the lights of Portsmouth.

When the auditions were held in November, Connie got the leading part of Rose Maybud. I was unsuccessful this time, but was quite happy to be back in the chorus again. We celebrated our first married Christmas together in the caravan with Connie's mum and sister.

In the February of 1954 Connie wasn't feeling very well. She also had a cough and decided to go and see Dr. Gibson. He was a bit concerned and sent her to the hospital for tests and an x-ray, which unfortunately showed that Connie had TB. Dr. Gibson arranged for her to go into the sanatorium in Hursley Road, Chandlers Ford. Unfortunately there was a waiting list of six weeks before she could get in. For that time she sat resting on the settee in the bungalow. Connie went into the sanatorium three weeks before Easter 1954, where she spent nine months being treated. She was fortunate as it was picked up early thanks to Dr. Gibson's expertise. Several new drugs had also started to be used. She also had the top of one lung collapse and when she came home in November she had to go to the hospital once a week in order to maintain the air pressure. Over time this was gradually eased off and after two years she was given a clean bill of health, which was wonderful and Connie came back into the chorus of the opera.

When Connie was at Hursley Road she was visited by the Rev. Williams from Hyde and in conversation she said she was concerned that I was missing playing cricket because I visited her on Wednesday afternoons and also Saturdays and Sundays. He said *"Why not join the Hyde Fellowship team"* who played in the park on Tuesday evenings. After evensong on the following Sunday I saw Alan House, who was their secretary and responsible for running the team. I joined them the following Tuesday evening and played for the rest of the summer. One evening we heard this very loud double explosion and had no idea what it could have been. It wasn't until some time later that we discovered it was the sound of the sonic boom of a plane going through the sound barrier.

Alan also encouraged me to join the club who met every Saturday evening in Hyde Parish Hall. They had a very mixed programme, which included table tennis, billiards, snooker, ballroom, old time and square dancing, talks, quizzes and play-reading. They did many other things in the parish, which included carol singing, a hobbies exhibition and parish holidays. They were also responsible for entertainment at the harvest supper. I especially remember one of these. It was at the time when the Rev. Williams was leaving Hyde to take up his new post as rector of St. Mary's in Southampton. Eric Manley had the idea of a story of a gang of seadogs making the journey from Winnall pier down the River Itchen to discover Southampton! The show was a great success, with many laughs on the way. There was a crossing of the line ceremony, with Rev. Williams playing King Neptune. The lads made a mock-up of a boat which they fixed on some pram wheels so that it could be pushed on to the stage. About four of us were in the boat and I was standing in the bows singing 'Blow the man down'. At the dress rehearsal the weight of the four men was too much for the poor pram wheels and they began to buckle and from the front it must have really looked as if we were going to sink and go down among the dead men, but it was all right on the night and we sailed on without mishap.

Rev. Williams was a very gifted man and was a good leader with the ability to delegate and lead from the front. It was very gratifying to know that someone with his talent did eventually get near the top in the Church, when he later became Provost of Coventry Cathedral.

Another thing the Fellowship did was organise group holidays. In August 1954 we joined four other couples for a week's holiday in Torquay. The couples were our friends Brenda and Alan, Alan's Mum and Dad, Mr. and Mrs. Burton and Mr. and Mrs. Knight. We travelled by National Coach, which we had to catch in Southampton. We then had to change coaches in Bournemouth and arrived in Torquay late on the Saturday afternoon. This was to be our first holiday together and the first holiday I'd had for about eight years, when I had stayed with Uncle Bill, Granny's brother in Emsworth. Holidays were another thing that suffered because of the war and the austere years after. Once we arrived in Torquay we made our way to the YWCA, where we were to stay. Our meals were cooked for us, but we had to help with the washing up and make our own beds and keep our rooms tidy. Nevertheless, the ten of us had a good time. Sometimes we would all go out together, at other times we would go out in groups. We often went with Alan and Brenda, as they were the only other young couple. We also went out on our own. One trip was the day we all went to the picturesque village of Cockington, where we had great fun. Alan's dad had a great sense of humour. Connie and I went on a boat trip up the River Dart as far as Dartmouth. We also went by bus to the fishing port of Brixham. In the evening we would go down to the front, sit in a double deckchair and throw pieces of bread to the seagulls as they flew by. We waited until it got dark to see the front lit up. We returned home on the Saturday and felt that we had had a good holiday and made some new friends. Today this sort of holiday may seem rather tame, but to us at that time it was a great change and after the setback of Connie catching TB it was another step on the road to a complete recovery.

By the autumn of 1955 Connie was well enough to rejoin the opera chorus for HMS Pinafore, which the Society was producing with Trial by Jury. I was fortunate to have a part in both, the usher in Trial and the bosun in Pinafore. We also had a new producer Gladys Starling, a really lovely lady who got the very best out of everyone. She always reminds me of that wonderful actress, Cicely Courtneidge. Connie gave up her solo singing, but carried on in the chorus.

About this time I had my first paid engagement, to sing at the Friary Bowling Club dinner. As this was to be a first I thought I had better get myself a dinner jacket, which I bought for twelve guineas. When I met the Friary secretary to discuss arrangements he said *"By the way, it's informal"*. Never mind, the jacket did come in handy for many years after. They must have liked me, as about three weeks later I was asked to sing at the Hyde Abbey Club dinner. I sang at the Friary again the following year and for many years after. When I said that I'd run out of songs they said *"Sing the old ones"*, they seemed to like the ones they knew.

We carried on going to evensong at Hyde after Rev. Williams left. The new vicar was Rev. Wells, who was also a very good musician and pianist. He very often played for the concerts and other events held by the Fellowship. He also played for me on several occasions. The Fellowship continued their varied programme. They held a very successful hobbies exhibition and had a varied list of speakers. I talked for them once about beekeeping. They also came round the nursery a couple of times, when we would finish up with refreshments on the lawn.

By 1955 Granny was finding it difficult in many ways living on her own in the big house, so she decided to move out and go and live with Aunt Flo in Uplands Road at Weeke. Dad decided to move into the old house and we agreed to rent the bungalow off Dad. The question then was what we were going to do with the caravan. We tried to sell it, but had no luck. Lincoln Gear, who ran a couple of permanent caravan sites, including the one in North Drive, agreed to let it for us on a site in Sutton Scotney. The income from it more than paid for the rent we were paying Dad for the bungalow.

About this time John's marriage fell through and he was divorced from Margaret. It was all rather sad, they just didn't seem to have any interests in common. Margaret had her square dancing, needlework and Red Cross activities, John had his love of cricket and trains. I remember taking Mum up to Whitchurch to see Margaret's Mum, but I think they felt unable to help and eventually they just went their own way.

Moving from the caravan to a bungalow meant we had to purchase furniture, some of which still had the war time utility mark on it. Moving to the bungalow meant I was moving back to the home where I was born and brought up. It seemed a bit cold and bare after two years of living in a cosy caravan. We set to decorate it in bright and warm colours. Mum was very fond of cream, so all the paintwork was cream. We painted the bedroom ceiling primrose, with different paper on one wall to the others. This, we thought, was in fashion. We also painted the front door a bright yellow.

After an interregnum of two years, Littleton and Crawley at last got a new rector, the Rev. Dennis Earle, who came to live with his family in the rectory at Crawley. He had been a curate at St. Cross. He hadn't been a rector for very long when, one day, he paid us a visit at the Nursery. In conversation he expressed concern about the yew tree in the churchyard. He said the branches were so low over the path up to the church that when a coffin was carried up the path the branches were brushing the flowers off the top of the coffin. He wondered if we could give advice about cutting it back. I said I would have a go at it myself. We arranged to meet one Saturday afternoon and when I arrived he had obtained a long ladder, which we pushed up into the tree. I went up the ladder while he held it. When we were half way through the job, he volunteered to go up himself, but I managed to dissuade him, as he wasn't a young man like me. We finished the job in the afternoon. He impressed me with the fact that he was willing to have a go himself, so he deserved our support.

A little while after this we decided that we should support our own church and so made up our minds to leave Hyde, where we had been made most welcome, and return to our own village church. The Rev. Earle was very good at visiting parishioners and getting round the village and within a short time the congregation began to increase. With the help of Mrs. Earle and one or two other ladies he got the Sunday school going. Mrs. Jefferies, who was a music teacher at St. Swithun's School, took on the post of organist. She also formed a small choir of boys and girls. After evensong on a Sunday night she had a little feature where she got one of the girls or boys in the choir to sing a verse of a hymn after the service from the vestry. The congregation would wait and listen. After one such time I said to her *"Who was that who sang tonight, he had a nice voice"*, she replied *"Don't you know, it was your brother Richard"*.

Morning and evening services were now being held every Sunday, with the help of two lay readers, Mr. Pitney in Littleton and Mr. Wright in Crawley. We gradually became more involved. The Rev. Earle had been a curate at St. Cross before he came to Littleton, where they had a very successful church fellowship, so we discussed whether we had enough people to start one here. We asked round the church members if they would be interested and got a positive response. The decision was made to have a go and we formed a small committee of adults to run it. We based it much on the lines of our experience at Hyde. We would meet in the village hall every other Saturday evening with the aim of taking the church to the people. The idea was that from 6 o'clock until 8 o'clock would be a time for the youngsters, with table tennis, darts, billiards and board games. At 8 o'clock the adults would join us and we would then have a talk, any questions, lantern slides and dancing. We went round the village carol singing at Christmas, finishing at Brigadier and Mrs. Henderson's at Monks Rest for mince pies and rum coffee. We had summer evening picnics at Farley Mount. One of the speakers we had was Mrs. Temple, widow of Archbishop Temple. She was very involved with the prison and prisoners' welfare.

We started the first harvest supper and tried to make the old hall look as much like an old fashioned barn as we could. We had bales of straw round the sides to sit on. I don't expect that would be allowed today. On the wall we had rakes, hoes and scythes and on the stage we had an old horse hoe. All the implements we had borrowed from Mr. Maddrell at Harestock Farm, which was about where Priors Dean Road meets Harestock Road now. Right down the middle of the hall we had bare wooden tables. I can't really remember exactly what the food was, I expect it was the traditional cheese, potatoes and salad followed by apple pie. Entertainment was supplied by the members themselves, the boys and girls did a series of small sketches. One girl was being taught ballet. Mr. Clinton, the church warden and village road man, told some jokes. He wasn't really very funny, but everyone laughed and joined in the fun. I learnt one or two songs connected to the countryside. They seemed to go down very well and I continued singing them at concerts and dinners for the rest of my singing days. Rob Wilton, my pal from the opera, came as a guest and sang. We finished the entertainment by singing Offenbach's gendarme duet. The entertainment was followed by dancing, usually of the old fashioned type. The evening would be finished by the Rev. Earle with a prayer.

At that time the holding of the harvest supper by the church was a comparatively new idea. They had always been traditionally held by the farmers for the farm workers after the end of harvest. A harvest supper has been held by St. Catherine's Church every year since, which is now over 50 years.

At one committee meeting a lengthy discussion went on as to membership and whether it should be restricted to members of St. Catherine's Church only. After a long discussion it was decided that if we were to take the church to the village, it should be open to everyone. We eventually had members who belonged to other churches and denominations and those who belonged to none. At Easter we performed a Passion play, which Mrs. Quinton, who lived at Crawley, produced. She was quite professional and really got the best out of everyone. I played the small part of one of the disciples one year and being part of it and the meaning of Easter and the crucifixion, for me, became a reality. Most of the cast had very little or no experience of acting, yet the whole meaning and experience of being part of it brought out the characters of the part they were playing. One person was Mr. Adams, who lived at St. Swithun's Cottage. He had never acted in his life before and was playing the part of Peter. He got into it and felt the part so much that he gave the effect that he really was Peter.

Another very successful event we held was a hobbies exhibition. This covered a very wide range of interests. Among them were some documents brought by Mr. Wardle, who lived at St. Swithun's, now The White House. He had been a prisoner of war in the infamous Colditz prison. He brought some of the false documents and passes made by the prisoners to help them escape. On the stage Rev. Tanner had an exhibition of old Littleton photographs and in the evening he gave a talk with slides of the history of Littleton and Harestock. Mervyn Merwood, one of the teenage members, was a very keen young gardener and suggested the idea of holding a flower show. He put the idea to the committee and said he would be prepared to take on the job of secretary. It was decided to have a go and hold a small show in the village hall on the first Saturday in September. A schedule was drawn up and Mervyn went round the village door to door selling them. He was really keen. I remember feeling rather anxious as the day drew near as to whether we would get much support in the way of entries. I needn't have worried. When the day arrived we had over 250 entries, which far exceeded our expectations. It was great credit to the work Mervyn had put in. He also got certificates and sponsorship money from different firms. To raise money to fund the show a small fete was held on the Rec. Among the stalls was bowling for the pig. The following year, 1957, we hired a marquee in which to hold the flower show and used the hall for teas. It was a great success once more, with even more entries, again with Mervyn putting in a lot of hard work. Unfortunately after the show Mervyn said he would no longer be able to carry on as secretary as he was leaving. I think it was to go to university. We tried to get someone to take on as secretary, but were unable to do so. After two successful years the show fell through, not because of lack of support, but because we were unable to get someone in the Fellowship to take on the job of secretary, but we had sown the seeds which were to emerge some 12 years later.

One happening I do remember with the Fellowship was when we gave a group of teenage youngsters some money to go to town to buy records which we could use for dancing to on Fellowship evenings. When they came back they were looking rather guilty. When I asked them what they had been up to they said that among the records they had bought was one of the Goons, the Ying Tong song, which was very popular at that time. Nowadays if I just happen to hear it it always reminds me of that time and what a smashing lot of youngsters they were. I can still see them all laughing when they played it. If I happen to meet any of them now, some 50 years later, they still talk of the fun we had in the Fellowship.

By 1957 Connie had no longer to go to hospital for check-ups. She had been given a clean bill of health and made a complete recovery from TB, which was wonderful.

I have a rose, the perfect rose
A rose God picked for me
A lovely rose, the sweetest rose
That flowers eternally
I love this rose, this perfect rose
This rose from a heavenly tree
This happy rose, this shapely rose
Thank God she married me

Written by Bob Riley, a rose grower, and pinned up in his greenhouse for his wife Josie to find.

"Yum Yum marries Pish Tush"

Our new caravan and home on the nursery site

Coronation carnival procession through the village

Granny and Grandad, photo taken a week before Grandad died

Our first holiday away together at Torquay with the fellowship we are on a boat trip on the River Dart

St Catherine's church fellowship hobbies exhibition opened by Rev Tanner L-R: George Smart, Rev Tanner, myself and Mr Pitney

Church fellowship flower show, 1956, Mrs Adams, Connie, Mervyn Merwood, Mr Aylin, Mr Crimble

Tape 11
Family Life

On Sunday 26th January 1958 David, our eldest son, was born at the Royal Hampshire County Hospital. Unlike today, fathers were not welcome at the birth, so I had to wait at home, although I did visit Connie in hospital on Saturday evening, when I was told I would have to ring in the morning to see if there were any developments. As we didn't have a telephone of our own at the time, the following morning at about 8 o'clock I had to go to Mum and Dad's to ring up the hospital. I was told by a nurse that we had a baby daughter. I immediately told Mum and Dad that they had a granddaughter, when the phone rang and it was the nurse I had just spoken to, full of apologies saying it wasn't a daughter, it was a son! Visiting was only allowed at certain times, but as it was a Sunday I could go in the afternoon, which I did, picking up Connie's Mum on the way. When we arrived, Connie was on the veranda of the hospital which had a lovely view overlooking Winchester College and St. Cross. David was in a cot beside the bed. He was a very bonny baby of 10½ lbs with a lovely complexion. I think Connie had to stay in hospital for about 10 days or a fortnight, which would have been the norm at that time.

We brought David home and put him in a wicker cradle decorated with muslin, lent to us by Hilda Herridge. She had used it for her children and it was now being used by most of the new mums in the village. I also remember her saying *"Enjoy them while they are babies, because they are not like that for long. If you have to get up in the night, make a cup of tea and make the most of it!"* We did have a home help for a couple of weeks, who did the washing and kept the place clean. Within a few weeks and as the days got longer and warmer, Connie was taking David out in his new pram, meeting up with the other new mums in the village.

I didn't join the opera the year David was born, so for the winter months I joined the Caer Gwent Male Voice Choir. Some of the men in the Opera belonged. My friend Rob was the chairman. I had always enjoyed the sound of a male voice choir and it was a great experience singing with them.

David very soon outgrew his cradle and was moved into his new cot. On Palm Sunday he was christened by the Rev. Earle and was dressed in the family christening gown passed down on the Goater side of the family. His Godparents were John, Rob and Connie's friend Margaret. It was a very wet day and the photos had to be taken in the porch of the bungalow.

Within a year David was walking and within two years he was running round the nursery. We had a fright one day. Mum was looking after him, but when she turned her back for one minute he fell into a water tank. Luckily there was only about six or seven inches of water in the bottom and by the time she got to him he was standing up looking over the side. It didn't put him off going into the water, which he always enjoyed doing.

On Sunday 5th February 1961 our second son, Andrew, was born at the Royal Hampshire County Hospital. Again I had to wait at home, this time it was the Monday morning when I rang the hospital and again I was told I had a daughter. I informed Mum and Dad that they had a granddaughter, and I went to work as I was not allowed to see the baby and Connie until the evening. I spent all day telling everyone we had a daughter. When I saw Connie in the evening and said *"Well, we have one of each"* she replied *"What do you mean?"*. When I said that I had been told that we had a baby girl, she replied she had been told we had a son. Unfortunately it had not been an easy birth and baby Andrew had been kept in the baby unit and Connie had not seen him. She called a nurse and told her what I had said, to which the nurse replied *"It's a boy, you had better come and see for yourself"*, which I did. The nurse said I must have misheard, but I'm sure it's not a thing that could have been misheard, especially after what had happened when David was born. I know it is often said that truth is stranger than fiction, but this is exactly what happened.

By this time David was such a fine little boy and full of energy that when I saw baby Andrew he looked so small and pale I said to Connie that we would need to give him extra care. I needn't have worried, however, as within a few years he too was a fine little boy, full of energy and well capable of looking after himself. John's son, Nigel, was born a fortnight after Andrew and we had a combined christening in the spring and gathered at Mum and Dad's house for a christening party. Andrew again wore the family christening gown.

At that time the family seemed to be all boys. Our cousins Maurice, Gerald and Bill also had boys and boys seemed to be the majority in the village, so there were plenty of birthday parties to go to. The boys were growing up on the nursery very much in the same way I did, so I felt I was able to keep a step ahead of them in what they were up to. It wasn't until they grew up and told me what they actually did do that I realised that I wasn't as far ahead as I had thought.

One day I visited my cousin Gerald who lived in Hilden Way, he showed me the small pool he had built in his garden for his boys, Graham and Kevin, to play in. When I got home I dug a hole about six foot across and two foot deep, lined it with polythene sheeting and filled it with water. The boys were soon in it and having great fun on very hot days. I got in it with them sometimes. I kept it clean by siphoning out the old water and replacing it with new. We had a very good water supply on the nursery so it wasn't a problem. This small amount of water was such a success with the boys it gave me the idea of building a proper pool. I read articles by people who had built their own and decided to have a go. I was still playing cricket for Hyde Fellowship on Tuesday evenings and one of the team worked for a firm who were building merchants. He said he would help me with building materials. During the following winter I would spend about an hour every evening digging the hole. As the ground sloped away from the bungalow it meant that I dug down one end and built up the level at the other. I wouldn't have to dig as much as it appeared and went for making it longer rather than wider. It was a good job that we didn't have any close neighbours or they might have wondered what I was up to, digging a hole in the dark! I dug a hole 25 foot long by about 8 foot wide. I purchased most of the materials from my friend from the cricket and started on the job of laying the base and foundations for the walls. I had to mix all the concrete by hand. The walls consisted of hollow concrete blocks with reinforcing bars up the centre of the blocks which had to be filled with concrete. This was a little job the boys liked doing. They filled each hole using a small trowel and then tamped it in. I had never laid a concrete block in my life before. I then had to plaster the wall with a rendering mix, with a substance to make it waterproof. I found this the most difficult job of the lot and remember saying that when I had finished I would throw the trowel as far as I could. I then had to paint the walls with a blue waterproof paint. We then concreted about two foot around the side. The pool was quite near the bungalow, which was on one side, and at one end there was a beech hedge. On the other two sides we put up a fence for safety reasons.

The big day came to fill up the pool. We were very apprehensive that it might leak, but we needn't have worried, it was OK and the boys were very soon enjoying it. Lots of their friends also joined in, but we had to have very strict rules. They were not allowed in unless either Connie or myself were there and there was no pushing in or throwing in of anyone. They were very good, we never had any trouble, and the first year about eight or nine boys learnt to swim. The whole thing cost me just over £100. The best £100 I think I ever spent. It was large enough to be able to swim up and down and on hot summer days I would have a cool off in my lunch hour. It took a time to look after and make sure the chlorine and PH levels were correct. I did try to make my own filter with a pump and a dustbin full of gravel and sand, but it was never very successful so we had to change the water when it became too cloudy.

After a couple of years we put a polythene greenhouse over the pool and its surround, which kept the water temperature up. It also meant we had a longer season when we could swim and felt much warmer when we got out.

In the mid-1950s I had been churchwarden for about three years. My fellow warden was Mr. Lemon who lived at Westholme and was the Chief Constable of Hampshire. He covered the morning service and I the evening, which worked well because I had to work on most Sunday mornings. One of my successors was George Wadsworth, who had plenty of energy and in 1960 he joined the Parish Council. The Council had not been very active for the last few years. It seemed that when the war finished the community spirit, which was so strong during that time, gradually diminished and it became difficult to get people to serve on the Council. Those few who did were the old parishioners who just kept things ticking over. One evening after evensong George approached myself and Bill Maltby as to whether we would consider joining the Council. He had now been made chairman. We both agreed to give it a go and as the numbers were below the required amount, we were co-opted.

The first big job that needed to be done was to improve the heating in the village hall. The hall itself was a bit like a large barn. To do this it was necessary to put in a false ceiling and improve the insulation. The hall needed to be completely re-decorated. I don't think this had ever been done since the hall had been built. All the heating consisted of was a coal burning stove half way along the side of the hall. In the winter you either got cooked if you happened to be sitting near it, or frozen if you were near the door. Electric heaters were put in around the top of the walls, although these were never very successful and were expensive to run and not very efficient. One great advantage George had was that his job was supplies officer for the Royal Hampshire County Hospital, which meant that he had a large number of contacts and was able to purchase many materials at a reduced price. He got a paint supplier to give a very elaborate colour scheme to the hall, which we had to modify considerably. He was very ruthless when it came to a deal. I once gave him all the details of how to make up his own lawn sand. A few days later when I met him he said *"By the way, I got all those materials from SCATS, they were cheaper than you"*. As chairman of the Council he certainly believed in making a penny do a pounds worth of work.

In the early 1960s I started to get a problem with Lincoln Gear and the letting of our caravan. There had been a small smouldering fire in the kitchen and I went to Sutton Scotney to see him and inspect the damage. During the discussions he said he would see if he could get me a pitch on a holiday caravan site in Swanage, but he would need to do the van up before it went. I said *"Get me the site and then we'll talk about doing it up"*. Once he had obtained the pitch I said I would do it up myself. I felt justified in making this decision as he had been less than frank with me on several occasions. I got the van back on the nursery and spent the late winter and early spring doing it up. We took out the stove and fireplace, as these would not be needed during the summer season when it would be in use. We painted it inside and out. We got new mattresses, upholstery, bed-linen, pots and pans and cutlery and everything to make it comfortable and convenient and by early April we had it towed to Swanage. The following weekend we loaded up with all the cutlery and pots and pans and made off to Swanage. When we arrived the site was an old Purbeck stone quarry on the hill overlooking Swanage. The caravans were placed at different angles over the site. We made ourselves known to the Hancock brothers, who were the owners. They had both been quarrymen and stonemasons. They showed us where our van was. It was a lovely spot. When we were sitting having our meal we looked right over Swanage to Ballard Down with the cliffs and the sea to our right. We could also see the little steam train running along the Swanage railway below us. This was before it had been closed by Mr. Beeching. The site had a small shop selling a range of goods. There were a couple of toilet blocks and showers. If the calor gas ran out all we had to do was tell Mr. Hancock, who lived in a bungalow at the entrance, and he would replace it. Our idea was that we would have a holiday in it in the summer when the boys were not at school and perhaps have a weekend or two. The rest of the time we would let it to friends in the village and locally. This would help to pay for the site. We didn't have any problem doing this, the first summer it was occupied most of the time. I think most of the people also enjoyed it. We still have the visitors' book which has some very nice comments in it.

The boys always enjoyed going to Swanage. The first thing they would say when we arrived was *"Let's find some friends"*. It was a great place for boys to play as it was an old quarry and was uphill and down dale with many nooks and crannies to explore. Andrew gave us a fright when he was quite small. He disappeared over the edge of a small sloping cliff. I ran round expecting to see him hurt, but before I got there he was running round the corner to meet me. I think he must have just rolled down like a ball. When we stayed for the week during the summer holidays, during the day we would usually go round to the beach at Studland. This was in the old days when it belonged to the Banks family, before it had been handed over to The National Trust. It was much less organised than it is today, with far less people. We parked in the sand dunes and sometimes got stuck. It had been used during the war for practice for the D Day landings and one day we had to keep clear of an area where an unexploded shell had been found. When we came back to the caravan about 4 o'clock Connie would prepare a meal while the boys played around the site. In the evening they loved to go down to the front at Swanage crabbing. The first time Andrew put in his line with bait on he must have pulled out one of the largest crabs along the front. Before we went home they were all tipped out of their bucket into the sea. I'm sure when we went back the next night the same ones were pulled out again. I think the crabs must have got used to it.

The first winter we had to remove the caravan and bring it back to the nursery and then take it back the following spring. By the second season I had got to know Mr. Hancock quite well and he said he was glad I had taken over the site from Lincoln Gear and I was welcome to leave it there the following winter. We had some lovely holidays in Swanage while the boys were growing up. Holidays that we might not have had had it not been for the caravan. I think the boys still look on Swanage as their second home.

Both the boys went to Crawley School, much the same as John and myself had done some 30 years before. The toilets had been brought up to date and they had their own dinner cooked for them there in their own kitchen. They still had three teachers. Miss Crosby the headteacher, who I knew through the Operatic, Miss Davey, a rather large lady who seemed to tower over the children and Mrs. Stone the infant teacher who was very much loved by the younger children. When I went back after all those years it all seemed so much smaller than I remembered. I was asked by the Littleton Parish Council if I would be their representative on the Board of Managers. I found it interesting and I later became its chairman.

Unlike myself, both the boys did well at school. David went to Montgomery of Alamein School, which was a great school at that time with a wonderful headmaster, Dennis Beacham. David was a prefect and captain of his house. He then went on to Peter Symonds, which was being changed from a grammar school into a sixth form college. He then did a horticultural degree at Reading University before joining Hilliers, like his grandfather had done 70 years before. He is now a manager of their Braintree unit producing some two million shrubs in containers. Like his grandfather he likes to be hands-on.

Andrew took a slightly different route when he left Crawley. He went to the brand new Henry Beaufort School in Harestock, being in the first intake. They were lucky in that first year as there were only about 250 children and were taught by most of the new heads of department. Andrew and his friends all seemed to do very well. Andrew went on to Peter Symonds, which was now well established as a sixth form college. He worked hard and gained a place at the Royal Veterinary College training as a veterinary surgeon. We dropped him off on a dark, wet Sunday evening in October at his digs in Tavistock Square in London, which seemed so different to the area around Littleton where he had been brought up. Both boys gained their degree, David after three years and Andrew after five, the last two years he spent at the Veterinary Centre at Potters Bar. His first job was with a vet's practice in Pulborough in Sussex. I always tell the tale that if I meet an old schoolfriend and tell them about the boys they say *"Who did you marry?!"*

The one thing we do have in common is our love of the countryside. From an early age they liked to go out into the country. We would go to several of the local shows like Romsey and the New Forest. One of the things we especially liked to attend was the county ploughing match, which was usually held in

November. Connie and myself would spend our time watching the horses ploughing and the boys would go off to inspect all the farm machinery, both new and old.

One year they had a gyro tiller which had been renovated. It was as big as a steam engine with large rotors on the back which stirred up the ground. It was driven by a diesel engine. They were used during the war to break up ground which had small trees and bushes on. I can remember seeing it used to break up Littleton Down, which was very overgrown. It turned up the rabbit burrows with the rabbits running in all directions. The boys liked to go out combine spotting during harvest time. They also liked to go out on their bikes, much the same as we had done. David liked to play tennis and Andrew his cricket.

In 1961 the Rev. Earle retired and his place was taken by the Rev. Philip Bell, who had been a parson on Tristan da Cunha. He always seemed quite active within the church and with the church people, but we didn't seem to see very much of him in the village. His eldest son, Michael, liked working on the nursery in his holidays in the summer. He would spend most of the time cutting the hedges around the nursery with a pair of Wilkinson Sword clippers. This was some job as we had nearly one mile of hedges if you counted both sides. When we sent the clippers in to be sharpened the following year Wilkinsons said that the clippers shouldn't have worn like that and they replaced them with a new pair. I don't think they really knew how much use they had.

Before he left Tristan da Cunha, Philip Bell collected seed from some of the native plants which he gave me to see if I could germinate them. The only one I can remember now was watercress, which I grew in a flowerpot without any water.

One of the most difficult times we had when the boys were small was the winter of 1963, which started on the evening of Boxing Day 1962. We had spent the evening with our friends Rob and his wife. About 9 o'clock when we made for home it had started to snow and we had quite a job to get the Morris van, which we were using, up the slope outside of Rob's house. We eventually got home and put the boys to bed. Little did we realise at that time that the snow would stay on the ground until about 4th March, when it started to melt. As the cold spell went on it became more difficult to keep the bungalow warm, as it had very little insulation. Our main means of heating were an open fire with a back boiler to heat the water and one radiator, an oil stove in the kitchen and electric heaters for the bathroom and bedrooms, which we couldn't afford to use too much. I spent quite a lot of time after work cutting up wood for the fire. We were about 150 yards from the main road and only had a half inch water supply. At the end of January this froze up and left us without any water. I had to use the nursery water barrel, which was on wheels, to collect water from Mum and Dad's house, which was near the road and still had a supply. We weren't the only ones in the village without water. Apparently when the Crabwood water supply was first put in, some of the pipework wasn't installed very deep and where the snow had been cleared the frost went into the ground deeper and froze the pipes. The water company even put an electric current through their pipes to try to thaw them. We discovered that our pipe had frozen at the entrance to the nursery where the snow had been cleared. With the help of Uncle Percy we dug out a new trench in the open snow covered ground, cut the supply above and below the spot where it was frozen, and by-passed it with a new supply which we made sure was deep enough and covered by snow.

The birds and the animals suffered even more than we did because of the cold and snow, which covered their food. I remember walking round under the fir trees in our little copse at the bottom of the nursery and picking up the pigeons which had fallen out of the trees overnight, starved and frozen to death. When we finished work at night the hares from the fields at the back would follow us up the path. They would jump on our glass cloches, which would have slightly thawed during the day, to get at the anemones which were still green underneath. We lost a large number of cloches.

The cold weather just went on and on and everyone would be watching the weather forecast hoping for signs of an end, which didn't come until 4th March. Along the far side of the recreation ground long drifts of snow had built up over the two months. When it did eventually disappear, the grass which had been underneath the drifts was yellow because of the lack of light. Poor David had been given a new bicycle for a Christmas present. He wasn't able to ride it out until March. It had to stay in his bedroom whilst all he could do was look at it and keep it clean. It was by far the worst winter I have ever experienced. When it did eventually ease it took a long time for the snow drifts to thaw. I think it is the only time I can remember when even the children were glad for it to disappear.

In the early 1970s the Hancock brothers sold their quarry caravan site to a large company. They started to make new restrictions concerning caravans on the site. I got a bit fed up with this and as our caravan was getting a bit old, over 20 years, we decided to give it up. For a couple of years after that our holidays were spent in rented chalets in Eastbourne and Dawlish. The last few holidays we had after that with the boys we spent in apartments. In 1975 and 1976 we rented a nice apartment at Babbacombe near Torquay. I shall never forget that we went on to Dartmoor one day. It was the very hot, dry summer of 1976. There had been no rain since spring and this was August and most of the leaves on the trees were turning brown, just as though it was autumn. The trees on Dartmoor were much worse than those around Littleton. That night I couldn't sleep worrying about what was going to happen to them. When we got back home from the holiday the Littleton trees were showing signs of turning brown, but still not as bad as those in Devon. There was a lot of speculation as to what would happen as this occurrence had not been seen before in this country. In many of the fields the grass turned brown and then almost disappeared. As it happened I don't think we need have worried as much as we did. Rains came in September and went on nearly until Christmas and in the fields the mushrooms came up in their thousands. The following spring the leaves appeared on most of the trees the same as usual. There may have been some dead branches here and there. Apparently the browning of the leaves was the tree's way of protecting itself by reducing the transpiration of moisture through them. The trees growing on the chalk coped better than those on other soils because the chalk acted like a large sponge, drawing up moisture from the underground aqueducts. Like the winter of 1963, the summer of 1976 is something I don't wish to experience again.

Since the boys have grown up Connie and myself appreciate a bit more comfort and spend our holidays in hotels, most have been either in Shanklin on the Isle of Wight, or Swanage.

What shall be done with autumn leaves? They were the grace and the glory of by-gone spring and summer; but now they litter the whole garden, and if allowed to lie there, will obliterate all trace of the care and labour bestowed on the ground. They may be treated in either of two ways; either they be dealt with as worthless rubbish to be swept up and burnt; or they may be garnered to form a fertilising mould for future seasons of flower and fruit. So it is with the memories of a passing life.   *Sir Herbert Maxwell*

Connie, myself with the boys

We built the swimming pool, the best £100 I ever spent. The boys enjoying the pool covered with a polythene greenhouse

Enjoying the wonderful beach at Studland

Andrew playing cricket with Dad and David on the recreation ground where the memorial hall now stands

David with his degree at reading university

Richard and David by the greenhouses – severe winter of 1963

Tape 12
The Growing Nursery

During the 50s the business gradually expanded and we started growing more flowers and bedding plants, which we were beginning to get a name for locally. We built another Dutch light double bay greenhouse 60' x 20'. It was made by Robinsons of Winchester. At that time they had a workshop in Eastgate Street. The greenhouse was made by just clamping the Dutch lights together. They also supplied the heater. This consisted of an oil fired boiler combined to an electric fan which circulated the hot air round the greenhouse. The heater was controlled by a thermostat. The flame in the heater was either on low or high, it never went out. Heating greenhouses with hot air was a new idea and it did mean some adjustment in growing methods. The main difference was the humidity of the air in the greenhouse and that plants also dried out quicker. One thing it did mean was no more having to stoke the boiler and clean out the ash. It also made it possible to keep an even temperature. I did have to sit up all night once when the company who supplied the oil inadvertently allowed water to become mixed with oil. It was a very cold night and the water kept freezing in the filter on the oil tank. I had to clean out the filter about every hour to keep the burner going. The house was full of tender plants which we would have lost if the frost had got in. By the morning the water which was in the oil had dropped to the bottom of the tank and was beginning to freeze. The company who had supplied the oil had to place a heater under the tank before they could pump out the oil and replace it with clean.

In the 50s, a new method of growing chrysanthemums began to evolve. This consisted of growing them directly into the beds in the greenhouse instead of growing them in pots. The rooted cuttings were planted directly into the soil about 6"-8" apart. This was done in July. They were then either allowed to flower one bloom to a plant or pinched out once they were established and then allowed to produce no more than three stems to a plant. This method would then produce flowers from October to December, depending on the variety. We tried this in our new Robinsons greenhouse, but without much success the first season, mainly because of a disease known as eelworm. This gradually worked its way up the plant, killing the leaves on the way. The method of producing cuttings had always been by cutting the plant down nearly to ground level, then taking the roots with a piece of stem, which was called a stool, then planting them close together in a box. The boxes we used were kipper boxes which we obtained from the fishmonger. A way of killing the eelworm had been discovered. If the stools were heated in water at quite a high temperature, I think it was about 170°F, for about three minutes, this would kill the eelworm. We got a 50 gallon water tank, put it on two piles of bricks, half filled it with water and heated it with a large flame gun which we used on the nursery for killing weeds. We made a wire basket to put the stools in and then put them in the tank in hot water for about three minutes, pulled them out, plunged them into cold water and then boxed them up. We had a pleasant surprise because it didn't only kill the eelworm; it also made the stools produce many more cuttings than they normally would have done.

One of my friends in the Operatic Society, Dick Trower, ran a firm called DrixPlastic. They were making covers for hay and straw ricks. The sheet of plastic was placed over the rick and covered with a large net. They were looking for different ways of using plastic sheeting, which was a comparatively new product at that time. He asked me if I had ever thought of using it to cover plants, which I hadn't, but thought it might be worth giving it a try. He gave me one of their covers to see what I could do with it. We had some odd pieces of wood about the nursery, mainly glazing spars taken out of old greenhouses. These gave me the idea of trying to make a greenhouse out of them. I took my shape from the sides and top of the Robinsons greenhouse. I found that if, instead of having the sides upright, I splayed them out slightly at the bottom about a foot, it made the structure far more rigid. The shape was more like a Bedouin tent in the desert. It also allowed the wind to blow up and over them. We fixed the polythene to the frame with inch wide battens. We then fixed it into the ground and covered the bottom of the side with soil. We were quite surprised at how rigid the whole thing was. This was just a prototype, we just wanted to see if it would work and not blow away. We hadn't even worked out how we would make the ends, so we left it there for a couple of months during the summer to see how it would stand up to the weather. This it did much better than expected. We planted a couple of rows of tomatoes under it and they grew reasonably well.

During the winter we gave it further thought. One of the problems was that the polythene only lasted the duration of the summer, by the autumn it began to turn brittle and break up. This made us realise we would have to somehow obtain the maximum use out of it. To do this we decided we would have to make the structure portable, like cloches, able to move it over different crops. We chose to make it in sections, 12' long x 8' wide and about 7' high in the middle. Each section was bolted to the next in four places. Each corner and the middle of the sides we left a piece of wood which was buried in a hole made in the ground to keep it rigid. We made two pieces with a door in the middle which we bolted on each end. The soil was then banked up round the bottom of the ends and sides, stopping the wind getting under. The first year we grew a crop of lettuce followed by tomatoes. We then moved it over the chrysanthemums in September. These had been growing outside during the summer.

There were one or two problems, the main one being lack of ventilation, which created mildew and damping off of the blooms. To help overcome this we built sliding ventilators in the sides. During the winter I built another one which was wider. I had always enjoyed working with wood. The following summer we tried using them for protecting other crops, like bedding plants.

My friend Dick Trower got very interested and brought a representative from ICI in to have a look at what we were doing. He informed us they were producing an improved plastic which would stand up to the sun's rays and last much longer and would last for over one year. I was a bit disappointed with our friends in the trade. They seemed to think it presented too many problems. Robinsons, the greenhouse manufacturers in Winchester, thought it was too flimsy and would blow away. I couldn't even get the people at the Horticultural Research Station at Lymington interested. I felt they almost laughed at us. I did, however, have a customer who was a bank manager who asked whether we had thought of patenting it. When I think now of how many poly-tunnels have been built, perhaps I should have taken his advice. Even Robinsons of Winchester were manufacturing and selling them a few years later. Each winter I would build another poly-house and in the very cold winter of 1963 I spent the time building two.

Building the poly-houses meant we needed more cultivated ground, so one Saturday afternoon in the winter a couple of men from the farm came down with their tractor and pulled out the old orchard. About the same time we bought our first rotovator, a Clifford 5 horsepower, which was quite large. Also it had a plough which could be attached. This meant we didn't have any more digging with a fork to do. I enjoyed ploughing with it; perhaps it was my memories of time on the farm as a boy following the horses ploughing.

With the extra production of the polythene greenhouses we were able to grow more crops than we could sell retail. The rotation of crops was lettuce and bedding plants in the spring, followed by tomatoes, one house of cucumbers and early flowering chrysanthemums. The polythene houses were then moved over a crop of autumn flowering chrysanths. We used Eltexoil stoves in the autumn, which we placed up the middle of the house, more to keep out the damp than to heat them. The lettuce we sold to Mr. Johnson, who had a wholesale vegetable business in Winchester. We were able to sell most of the bedding plants, tomatoes and cucumber either in the shop or on the nursery. The chrysanthemums we were able to sell through Helliwell and Co. of Southampton. We had been their customers for some time buying other flowers which we needed for the flower trade and floristry, which was still the most profitable part of the business.

In the early 60s Dad invited John and myself to join him as equal partners in the business. Dad and Grandad had both worked very hard in the past to grow produce to a very high standard and their policy had been to make the money and then invest it in the business, which meant a slow development. John and myself took the opportunity to go to evening classes held by the Horticultural Advisory Board at Eastleigh. Among the things we learnt was about making use of your assets to borrow money to expand.

About the same time the landlord of our shop in Parchment Street, George Nutter, died and we were given, as sitting tenants, the opportunity to buy it. Mrs. Nutter, his widow, said she was sure George would like us to have it, and we bought it from her for £1,750. It doesn't seem much now, but we had to borrow most of the money, principally through our solicitor, at a fixed interest. The first thing we did was to double the size of the shop. We took out the wall between the shop and the room behind. The wall consisted of large lumps of chalk laid on wooden boards at an angle, a sort of Hessian put over it and then plastered.

It was a wooden framed building and all the beams had been plastered over. This was removed to expose them. New oak supports were put in where the wall was taken out. Aubrey Harding was the architect and Joyces of Hyde were the builders. We were more than pleased with it when the job was done. With the oak pillars and beams it still looks very much the same today. While the work was being done, and to help the business to carry on, we rented an empty shop in Middle Brook Street.

In 1960 Richard left school and started work with us on the nursery. It could never have been very easy for him, having to work with two brothers who were nearly 20 years older than him. In the late 60s, when Dad retired, Richard joined us as a third partner.

Although the polythene greenhouses were proving quite profitable, they had two main drawbacks. The polythene only lasted at the most for two years before it was made brittle by the sun, and it wasn't economical to heat it, so they could only be used for about nine months of the year. We started to think about more permanent glass to replace it and we knew a nurseryman near Andover who grew chrysanths and had just built a new greenhouse by Robinsons of Winchester, so we went over to have a look. We agreed to get an overdraft from the bank and went ahead and arranged with Robinsons to build it. It was considerably bigger than anything we had built before, 60' x 40' double bay and 10' high in the centre of each bay.

One of the main problems we had building glass on the nursery was that the land sloped two ways, which meant the site had to be levelled. We did it by hand and it was some job. We planted it with half chrysanths and the other half with carnations, all directly into the soil. This meant three beds in each bay, one of chrysanths and the other carnations. Both the carnations and the chrysanths did well and within a year we had cleared the overdraft.

The government had been giving farmers grants for growing grain and also for farm buildings for some time and the nursery trade had been lobbying the government for grants for nursery buildings and greenhouses. They eventually agreed to a 40% grant on all new glass and nursery buildings. We decided to take advantage of this and built another identical house the following year. This time we had the footings and site levelled by machine. Over the next three to four years we extended both houses to 200' long and also built a single bay house 100' x 20'.

At that time the horticultural industry was changing and methods of production were very different to those when I started on the nursery. Chrysanthemums were no longer grown in pots over a long season with cuttings taken in February and March, they were now planted directly into the ground in beds 3' wide in July and, if they were to be for the Christmas market, they would be given artificial light for two hours every night, which made the plant think it was still a long summer day. This stopped the buds forming too soon. This may seem strange, but the chrysanthemum is what is known as a short day plant and the buds don't form until days become shorter and the nights longer. We left the lights on for about two hours every night from about August to September. Once the lights were turned off the buds would begin to form. The majority of the bloom would then be spot on for Christmas. The effect on carnations was the opposite to chrysanths. If we lit them in the winter, that made the buds form because they flowered in the summer when the days were longer.

Because of the large number of cuttings both of carnations and chrysanthemums that we now required, we weren't able to produce our own. These we now bought from other growers who did nothing but produce rooted cuttings for the trade. The carnation cuttings would arrive in the early summer and the chrysanths would come in over three weeks in July. To get them planted quickly was quite a big job. It meant all hands to the task. If it was hot weather I would start early in the morning at about 5 o'clock. I enjoyed the early morning with no one about, only nature. I remember one morning seeing the deer leaping through the long grass in the field next door, where Pitter Close now is. As soon as they were all planted we had to get the irrigation system on. This had been installed when the houses were first built. It consisted of a large tank holding several thousand gallons of water. This was then pumped by an electric pump to the irrigation system, which consisted of either an overhead sprinkler system or a ground level trickle system. We weren't allowed to put the whole thing directly on to the mains because we were adding liquid fertiliser to the water. All the different beds of carnations and chrysanths could be watered separately by solenoid valves connected through a control unit which opened and shut them and turned the pump on and off. The greenhouses were all heated by hot air connected to a thermostat which kept them at a required temperature. All this modern technology was OK when it was going well, but sometimes we had a breakdown. I had many sleepless nights just before Christmas when it was freezing hard and the houses were full of chrysanths for the Christmas market. We did later have a standby generator which we only ever had to use once. It was in the middle of the night, but once we got it going the electric was back on.

Although we had a good retail sale for flowers in the shop, most of the carnations and chryanths we grew at that time were sold wholesale. We supplied most of the flower shops in Winchester and in the surrounding district. The rest we sold through Helliwells, the flower wholesalers of Southampton. These had to be put in boxes, originally wood, which had to be returned. These were later followed by cardboard boxes. At Christmas it was a big job getting the flowers packed in the boxes and delivered to Helliwells for the early market. We would also be busy with our retail trade, which involved quite a lot of delivering work with our cars and van. Once they were old enough it was a job the boys liked doing at Christmas, going out in the van with John delivering the plants and flowers and sometimes getting a tip.

In 1967 the Royal Horticultural Society held trials at Wisley for new varieties of pelargonium, in which Dad decided to enter his geranium 'Crimson Crample'. He had found it as a sport, or mutation, on the scarlet variety 'Paul Crample'. As far as I can remember, it was just one shoot which produced the darker red and which he managed to root and keep fixed with the dark red. He soon built up a reasonable stock of it and it also proved to be vigorous, if anything more so than the parent 'Paul Crample'. In the spring he took six plants to Wisley, where they were planted out in the trial ground with about another 60 new varieties, also on trial. During the summer Dad went to see them growing and when he came home he said there were some wonderful new varieties of geranium, but when he walked into the ground and looked across he could pick out ours with the crimson red showing up. We had to wait until the autumn to get the results. When they arrived, Dad was over the moon, three new varieties had got the Award of Merit, 'Crimson Crample' was one of them, and the other two were won by the London Parks Department. Being one of three out of about 60 was a great achievement for Dad. There were no breeders' rights in those days, so we had to build up as big a stock of it as we could before we put it on the market, selling most of them to public parks, like Portsmouth and Southampton. It was a very strong grower and was perhaps too large for the private garden. I still keep a stock of them in my own garden likewise David and Andrew. They are a memory of Dad.

With the new big greenhouses we were able to grow more bedding plants, but we had a few problems on the way, mainly with getting the compost right. As we were having trouble with the germination of young seedlings, we changed from mixing our own and decided to buy compost in loads six yards at a time. All went well for a couple of years until we had a bad load and lost about 900 boxes of bedding plants. They replaced it with another load which we had analysed before use. This proved to be no good either. As we now had a more up-to-date soil sterilizer and had purchased a new 750 David Brown tractor with a front loader and a trailer we returned to making our own compost with our own recipe. We did eventually get compensation for our loss of plants thanks to the support of our A. D. A. S. officer.

As more people owned a car so we found more people coming on to the nursery to buy their plants. Dad had not encouraged this in the past, but now with the new idea of the garden centre where you just walked round and helped yourself to your requirements becoming popular we felt we had to open up to the public visiting the nursery. As people became more affluent and there was more money about they were able to spend extra on their garden. On the nursery we were able to display a larger range of plants than we could in the shop.

We also tried our hand at selling Christmas trees. I had a friend in the opera, Rita Stocks, who lived near Andover. They had several acres of land and were trying their hand at growing Christmas trees. When they were large enough we started selling them on the nursery and were quite successful and increased the sales every Christmas until the supply ran out and we had to find another supplier. I always felt selling Christmas trees was one of the easiest things we ever sold. We just stood them out round the nursery, people came in, picked out their own, paid for it and took it away. The only thing we had to be careful of was not to over-stock and have too many left after Christmas, when they are not worth anything. It was quite amusing watching people choose their tree. Some would pick up the first one of the right size that they found and others would go through every tree we had. The children seemed to want the largest one they could find, I'm sure some had to shorten the trunk when they got home. One Christmas a family of four, Mum, Dad and two children just couldn't agree and nearly came to blows. Mum and the daughter got in the car and went, leaving Dad and the son to walk home. What concerned us was they didn't even buy a tree. I don't know where the spirit of Christmas went.

In the late 60s we turned one of our sheds into a shop, which we stocked with some garden sundries. We had already turned part of Grandad's old stable and cart house into an office. With more and more customers coming on to the nursery in 1960 we made the decision to erect a new building consisting of shop, office, toilets and workshop. We were able to obtain grants for the last three, but not for the retail shop. To build it we had to knock down four of Dad's old greenhouses, which had been built before the war. We did leave the benches of one to provide a display area. We sub-contracted most of the work with Richard and myself doing the carpentry, the plasterboarding and the decorating. We started to call ourselves a garden centre, selling plants and sundries. Two or three years later we built an extension across the front which enabled us to stock more sundries and keep peat and compost dry. We divided responsibilities, with John covering the Parchment Street shop and deliveries, Richard the garden centre, and I took care of greenhouses and the growing of plants, although we were able to cover for one another. With the garden centre it meant we had to keep open weekends. We had a rota between the three of us. On duty one weekend, off the next and stand-by the next. We kept this rota for quite a number of years.

With the garden centre selling a large range of shrubs and herbaceous plants it meant we had to extend our horticultural knowledge. We were buying in shrubs from other nurseries to re-sell so we decided to have a go at growing our own. We set up a mist propagating unit in the small original Robinsons greenhouse. Once rooted they would be potted on and stood out in one of the large Robinsons houses. We cut back the growing of chrysanthemums and carnations for the wholesale trade, where the prices were gradually getting lower. I think with the grant the government had introduced there had been an over-expansion of the building of greenhouses which led to over-production. After a couple of years we stopped growing chrysanthemums and carnations altogether. We erected benches in the single bay Robinsons house, put in two heaters and lined it with bubble polythene so that we were able to keep the temperature up fairly high. We used this for germination and propagating bedding plants and for bringing on early bedding. In one of the large double bay houses we had two heaters to keep a moderate temperature. This was used for bedding plants as soon as they were pricked out. We also stood out all the geraniums in their different colours at the front and at the far end of the house we had all the baskets and containers we had made up. We liked to get them well established before they went outside. Many of these were the customers' own baskets and containers which they brought in every year to be re-filled. The other large house we filled with hardy stock which we were growing on. We sold the large heater which was in the middle of the house as it was no longer required. It had been in a concrete pit about 2' deep. This we fitted with a plastic liner and turned into a pond which we filled with water lilies and goldfish, which made a feature.

We found that customers liked to walk round the nursery and pick up the plants they required where they were growing. This meant that although I wasn't usually in the garden shop I met many of the customers as they walked round. I like to think that many of them over the years became friends, although I couldn't remember most of their names. One thing they all seemed to appreciate was the garden advice we were able to give them. We were lucky dealing with people who gardened as most of them were very pleasant and would seldom have any complaints. However, we did have one lady complain. She was a bit of an autocrat and always came in with her chauffeur, who she tended to talk down to. She always bought quite a few boxes of bedding plants. One year she came back, pushed in front of the customers in the shop and in a loud voice said that all the plants she had bought had died. I happened to be in the shop and started to question her as to what she had done with them. We had been selling hundreds of boxes during the season and hadn't had a single complaint. She replied that she knew all there was to know about gardening. My answer was that I had been working at it all my life and didn't know a quarter. She stomped out and said she would never come back again, but she did the following year and never said a word. Perhaps she found out what she had done. The most common answer in these circumstances was that the watering can had been used for weed killing and had not been properly washed out.

Business on the nursery grew, our busiest time being the spring, April, May and June, when we took half the year's income. We didn't have much time off during those three months, so I took my holiday at the end of June and almost gave a sigh of relief when I got on the ferry on our way to Shanklin on the Isle of Wight.

Although trade on the nursery was growing, the shop was not and was no longer paying its way, so we decided to cease trading as a florist shop. The idea was to do it up and let it. As it is a Class 2 Listed Building there were certain conditions we had to abide by. The upstairs, which we had used as storerooms, we turned into a flat. For the first 10 years it was let to three or four different people for either a children's shop or children's clothes shop. About 15 years ago Peter Ponsford Jones took it over as a clock shop, which it still is today. When we closed the shop John went over to running the garden shop, which is what we called it latterly, I carried on with the growing with some help from Richard, who also started doing some garden maintenance. Although Dad had given up his share in the business he kept a keen interest, still liking to do the cashing up every day and getting it ready for the bank. He kept his hand in and still liked taking cuttings when he **was over 90.** He was a really skilled nurseryman of the old school.

> *To watch the corn grow and the blossom set*
> *To draw hard breath over plough share and spade*
> *To read, to love, to hope, to pray*
> *These are the things that make men happy*

John Ruskin

The first polythene greenhouse we built

David on our David Brown 780 tractor

Rita standing out the boxes of bedding plants which had just been pinched out

Dad still keeping his hand in when over 90 taking dahlia cuttings

Richard, myself and John in the large greenhouse used for garden centre sale

Tape 13
From Opera to Television

All the operas performed by the Operatic Society during the 50s were by Gilbert and Sullivan and it wasn't until 1960 that the Society decided to make a change. I know Jack Sealey had been keen to perform something near to grand opera. We were now beginning to repeat some of the Gilbert and Sullivan operas we had performed since the war. I think the main concern was that other shows were more expensive to put on and Gilbert and Sullivan were more popular, some more than others, and audiences could be relied on. The Society decided to put on a new version of Johann Strauss' opera Die Fledermaus. It had just been arranged especially for amateur societies. It was to be something completely different for Winchester. The show called for a different style of acting and voice compared to Gilbert and Sullivan. I was fortunate in being given the part of Dr. Falke, the Bat, which called for a bass baritone voice, which suited me. When we arrived at the Guildhall for the first dress rehearsal and school performance the bookings were not too good. There seemed to be a doubt in the public's mind because it wasn't Gilbert and Sullivan and they weren't quite sure what it was all about. The first public performance on the Saturday, civic night, was always fairly well attended and this night the hall was about three quarters full. The show went very well and the audience were very appreciative at the final curtain. The following week the word must have got round and the audiences grew larger every night. One person I remember enjoyed it so much she went every single night.

Dr. Falke was by far the best part I ever had. I can still remember the wonderful feeling standing on the centre of the Guildhall stage singing 'Brother mine', supported by a chorus of about 50. We had a super cast led by Mary Spalding playing Rosalinde and Brian Cavel playing Eisenstein. We also had a wonderful producer in Gladys Starling. When we got to our dressing room after the last night, Brian said *"We shall never get a part like that again"*. How right he was. I did, however, play many parts after that, including Mountararat in Iolanthe, the pirate king in Pirates of Penzance; King Hildebrand in Princess Ida.

There is one incident which did happen which has nothing to do with the actual show. We were at the Guildhall getting ready for a schools' performance of La Vie Parisienne.

I had a small part in it, so I was changing in the principal men's dressing room which was situated in the minstrels' gallery over the banqueting hall, right at the top of the building. The fire alarm sounded, but no-one took any notice, only to say *"I expect it's a false alarm"*. We just carried on. Then someone said *"There's some smoke"*. We gathered our clothes and dashed down the stairs. When we got to the yard we saw that part of the Guildhall was on fire. So there was no show that night. I rang Connie to tell her I was OK, as it had been on the local radio and television that Winchester Guildhall was on fire. The fire was in a side building and didn't affect the main hall and we were able to perform the following evening.

The Society also started to put on a concert every autumn in the Guildhall. This was conducted by Felton Rapley who had come to live in Winchester. He may be remembered from the days when he played the organ on the BBC Radio. The concert consisted of numbers from some of the shows we had performed as well as some from musicals and grand opera. Some members also performed solo pieces. One year I was asked to do a couple of my songs with a rural flavour.

In the mid-60s Dorothy Crosby, Phyl Hamblyn, Norman Kennish, Reg Read, Rob Wilton and myself went to three WIs, Littleton, Crawley and Sparsholt, and sang a selection of numbers from Gilbert and Sullivan.

In the early 70s Ted Connolly, who lived in Littleton and was stage manager for the Opera, asked David, who was then about 12 or 13, if he would like to come and help backstage. So evenings when it didn't affect his school work, he came to the performance with me. He got very keen helping, and later also helped with the making of the scenery.

In the late 70s it was becoming more difficult for me to find the time to be in the show. The business and other commitments were taking more of my time. I also felt the standard of the show was not as good. The discipline of the singing wasn't what I'd been used to. I was content to be in the chorus for a couple of years and then decided to drop out the following year. About a year after, a fortnight before the show, I was asked if I could help them out. The person who was playing King Hildebrand in Princess Ida had been moved away from Winchester because of his job. As I had played the part in the previous production they wondered if I would step in. I only had ten evenings to swot it up. Thanks to the intensive rehearsing we had when I performed the part, it all came back in a few rehearsals. I wasn't going to take part the following year, but they were very short of men, so I took part in the chorus just to help out. It just didn't seem the same as it had been in years gone by.

That was my last show. I had been in the Society for over 30 years, for which I have a long service medal and bar. I owe a lot to the Society. I spent many happy hours rehearsing and performing. I had made many friends and, of course, I had met Connie. When I joined I wasn't a very confident young man. Being in the Society had helped my confidence in other walks of life.

The confidence I had gained was to be a great help to me with the turn my life was to take in May 1975. Like joining the Opera, it was something which came out of the blue. Gerry Way, whose wife once worked part-time at the nursery, often called in for plants etc. , a bit of gardening advice and a chat. One morning he brought in Bruce Parker, who at that time was the presenter of BBC South Today. He had just moved into a house in Lanham Lane, on the Winchester City border. Gerry was a friend of his and was giving him help and advice on his quite large garden. We got talking and I helped him with advice where I could. About a week later one of the staff called me to say the BBC was on the phone and they wanted to talk to me. When I got to the phone it was Bruce. He said they were going to do a gardening piece on South Today and call it 'Summer Gardens'. They were going to ask viewers to send in a picture, or slide, of their garden. They would then go out and film the garden, a piece which was to last about four minutes. The producer then wanted someone to give a comment on the garden shown and follow this up with tips on what we should be doing in the garden that week. He wondered if I would like to do this job. I took a deep breath and said I had never done anything like that in my life. I hadn't even given talks on gardening, like Dad had. I said I would see if I could find him someone. His reply was that he wanted me. He would come over and see me on Sunday morning. I can't remember really what happened that morning. I know I tried to wriggle out of it, but on South Today on the Monday evening they announced that they were going to do a piece on summer gardens every Thursday evening, which would be followed by gardening advice given by Austen Hooker. Bruce came over again before the Thursday and we talked over what I would do and say.

About 4 o'clock on the day I set off for Southampton, wondering all the way down what I had let myself in for. I arrived at the BBC, which at that time was situated in what had been the Great Western Hotel. I parked in the car park, which was where the platforms were for the old Great Western Railway terminal. It was where all the boat trains would have come in to embark their passengers for the great liners which departed from Southampton. They may have even stayed overnight in the hotel, with all its grandeur. I walked in and was told the BBC was on the first floor. I made my way up the grand marble staircase to reception, there I got someone to help me carry in the plants I had brought with me. Among them were tomatoes and growbags. I met Bruce, and was introduced to several of the production team. Among them was Don Osmond, the deputy editor. Don was better known as Oz, who did the cartoons in the Daily Echo. He had also drawn cartoons on South Today in its early days. I was taken into the studio where I was given a table to arrange the plants and growbag. I was then shown to the green room before going back into the studio for a rehearsal. I had my notes with me which Connie had typed. Bruce said *"Are you going to use those? It might be better if you let me have them. I have never let anyone dry up yet and you're not going to be the first."* So I gave him my notes, which he used to ask me questions. It worked very well, a system we carried on using. We ran through what I was going to do and say. It was not very long, roughly about three to four minutes. I was then taken back to the green room to wait for my time to go on. No-one was ever left on their own, there was always someone to talk to. I didn't get too nervous, I think my experience of going on stage in the opera helped. We sat and watched the programme going out on a monitor before I was taken back into the studio by the floor manager. I sat in my seat, my microphone was clipped on and waited for the gardening film to be shown, which Bruce introduced. We watched the film on a small monitor. I remember Bruce saying to me while it was being shown that he wished the colour on his set at home was as good as that, and I replied *"I wish mine was, because it's black and white!"*. When the film finished Bruce asked me what I thought of the garden. I passed some remark and we went into talking about the things to be done in the garden. I talked about support for tomatoes in growbags. It didn't seem as if we had hardly started when Bruce was thanking me and winding up. It had all seemed very different to appearing on the stage with a large audience. There was just Bruce, myself, two or three cameramen and a couple of other people. There was no sense of the large audience sat at home watching. I had to sit in my place until another piece of film was being used before I went back to the green room to wait for the finish. I was a bit surprised by the comment made by a member of staff who was sitting with me. She said *"They've got a good piece there, I hope they don't spoil it and mess it about."* When South Today finished, Bruce came round with several others. They all seemed quite pleased and I was asked if I was OK for the rest of the programmes. It was to be a six week run. I rounded up my things in the car and made for home, where everyone seemed to think it had gone alright. The only person who didn't watch was John. It was a repeat of his reaction when I had my first principal part in the opera. He couldn't stand the tension in case I made a mistake. It wasn't until I got home that the reality cut in, that I had actually appeared on TV. I must have had a high of adrenalin and just couldn't sit down. I had to walk round the nursery just to try and calm down.

I hadn't been back indoors long when there was a knock on the back door. It was a local friend, Dennis Brooks. It was to say that a past neighbour of his, Mrs. Duncan, who had lived in the village for many years, but now lived in Brighton, had rung him up to say she had just seen me on the television and would he give me her congratulations. I suppose it took me several days before I came down to earth, especially with customers coming in to the nursery who had seen it. After a couple more Thursday appearances I was beginning to get relaxed. I think one of the things I had learnt being in the opera was that no matter how many times you appear on stage, the nerves never completely go away. Bruce was always very good at helping me to relax by talking before we went on air. After about the third Thursday show he said he would be away for a fortnight and that Andrew Harvey would be fronting the programme the following week.

When I met Andrew before the programme he said he didn't know much about gardening, but Bruce had told him that I would tell him what to say. I think he meant I would give Andrew my notes, the same as I had been doing with him. It was also his way of giving me more confidence. When I went with Andrew to see the film of the garden which was to be shown, it was that of the lady who came into the nursery with a complaint who said she knew all there was to know about gardening. I passed some remark and Andrew said *"You're not going to say that, are you?"*. Actually I felt a bit sorry for her this time, as they had left it late to film her spring garden. All the spring flowers were over, so they had to film her old house instead.

Peter McCann stood in for Bruce the following week and the subject I was talking on was winter greens. He said he would just let me talk and wouldn't ask any questions unless he felt I needed any help, so I just talked through the programme. I could see him giving me the signal under the table when it was time to wind up. Bruce was back the following week and by that time I was beginning to feel more relaxed and enjoying my trip to Southampton every Thursday and I felt I would be sorry when the six weeks were up.

One evening before the programme Bruce asked me if I was interested in football, as they had Laurie McMenemy on the programme that evening. He said *"You'll be able to talk to him about football in the green room while you're waiting to go on air"*. When Laurie came in and I was introduced to him, before I could say a word he said *"Just the man. Now my tomatoes are better than Ted Bates'"*, his predecessor at The Dell. He spent the rest of the time talking tomatoes and I never got a word in about football.

When I arrived on the sixth week I had a pleasant surprise when I was told that they wanted to carry on with 'Summer Gardening' as it had proved very popular. I was then asked if I would like to be in some of the gardens when they were filmed. The first I attended was the local garden of Gerry Way. Frank Henning was the BBC reporter who was doing the interviews and he would ask me to pass comment as we walked round the garden. The series eventually finished in the autumn having run for 16 weeks. I had a very nice letter from Michael Harmen the editor, thanking me and saying they would like to make use of my services from time to time in the future.

It had been a wonderful experience being on the programme. Perhaps because we see the presenters on our television screens at home every evening we tend to think they are different from the rest of us. Working with them I realised they are all part of a team. Just the same mixture of characters like the members of any cricket team. I did get asked to appear again on several occasions, especially at Christmas and Mothering Sunday, and sometimes if they had a slot to fill in on the programme. Very often they gave me very short notice, being rung up about mid-day to do a piece at 6 o'clock. The advantage of gardening is there is always something to talk about.

One day in the autumn of 1978 I had a phone call at about 3. 00 p. m. from the studio. Could I help them out? James Callaghan, the Prime Minister, was thought to be going to make an announcement that there was to be an election in the autumn and was expected to talk for about ten minutes. At the BBC they had just heard that he'd now changed his mind about an election and would only be talking for about five minutes. This had not been confirmed, so they were in a fix as to how they could fill in the extra five minutes. They asked if I would go to the studio and stand-by. It meant I had to tear round and change, at the same time planning what I would talk about if required, get Connie to type my notes, and drive down to Southampton. As many may remember, Callaghan did change his mind and I filled in the five minutes. I remember when the programme was over, Don Osmond said to me *"You will always be able to say you appeared on the television in place of the Prime Minister"*. My claim to fame!

An amusing incident that happened was when South Today introduced an item which I think they called 'People's Programme', when viewers who had anything unusual could come into the studio and talk about it. The programme rang me to say they had a rather old lady who had this amaryllis which was about 32" tall and she wanted to know if it was a record. They said she was rather old to talk about it on her own and would I come in and interview her about it. I went in and met the lady and saw the amaryllis. It was very tall, like a green stick of rhubarb with an orange trumpet flower on the end. We had a rehearsal in the studio where we sat by the side of a small table with the amaryllis stood on it. She had really done everything wrong, by placing it in the darkest part of the room on top of a radiator. The situation was different for me. Instead of being interviewed, I was the interviewer. It was to be recorded, not live. As they were not ready we went into the green room and had a cup of coffee. While we were sat there talking with several other people I saw one of the cameramen come in looking rather sheepish. He came over to me and whispered in my ear *"We've knocked it off the table and broken it in half. But it's alright, we've stuck it together with Sellotape"*. So we went back into the studio and recorded the piece with the amaryllis done up with Sellotape! The old lady didn't seem to mind. I think all that mattered to her was that she was on the telly.

I did occasionally get recognised. I got the sort of look sometimes of *"Now where have I seen him before?"*. However, one day a lady came up to me in the old

International Stores in Winchester. She said *"Are you Austen Hooker, the one who does gardening on South Today?"*. Then she went on *"Are you the same one who sings in the opera in the Guildhall?"*. *"Yes, I am the same one"* I replied. I don't think she could believe that someone who was a gardener could possibly be able to sing in the Operatic Society. She then said *"Can I have your autograph?"*

One great thing about living in a village community is there is no chance of being big-headed. You may be a television and radio celebrity to the general public, but to people in the village you are still the same old Austen Hooker who lives on the nursery and plays cricket for the village team.

Although Bruce Parker presented South Today, he also sometimes sent tapes of interviews he had done up to the BBC in London, mostly for use on the John Dunn Show on Radio 2. One day he rang me and said that the John Dunn Show was looking for someone to do a garden piece. They were looking for somebody different. What did I think about sending up a couple of tapes? We made two tapes, one in his garden and the other in one of our large greenhouses on the nursery. Bruce sent them up to Broadcasting House, but after about a week we still hadn't had any reply. Bruce rang me and said he would ring them and find out what was happening. Five minutes later he phoned back to say that it was a studio based programme so they didn't want him, but they wanted to know if I would go up to London and record them with John Dunn. I felt rather awkward about this after all the help Bruce had given me, but he was adamant that I took the opportunity to go and he would confirm my acceptance.

The following day I received a phone call from John Malloy, the producer of the John Dunn Show. We fixed a time to meet John Dunn and make the recording. He also gave me, the country boy, instructions as to which underground to get on, which station to get off and directions to the BBC. When I reached the BBC buildings and looked at the famous well known front and doors that so many famous people had walked through, it gave me rather mixed feelings. I remembered reading Fred Streeter's book about how he felt the first time he arrived to do his famous radio gardening. He talked about walking up and down before he could pluck up courage to go in. I didn't walk up and down, but it did make me feel rather nervous and humble. I went through the doors and walked up to the reception and was told to take a seat, John Malloy was on his way down to meet me. I sat there watching people come and go, among them many were well known and famous. The person next to me was the actor, I don't remember his name, who took the lead in the 'Onedin Line'.

When I met John Malloy he said we were recording in a studio over the road, not in the main building. The BBC seems to use most of the buildings around there. I met John Dunn and was introduced. When you meet or see a photo of someone you have heard on the radio many times they are never as you imagined, especially when they are 6'7" tall! They said they were sorry they couldn't use Bruce as it was a studio based programme. As the programme went out every evening between 4. 00 and 6. 00 p. m. , the idea was to give listeners a few tips every Friday evening on what they could be doing in the garden at the weekend. John liked the way I had been doing the programme with Bruce by giving him my notes which he used as questions. He agreed that that was the way we would do it. The morning went well and we recorded four pieces to be broadcast, the first that evening and the others the following three Fridays. When we had finished recording they took me to the BBC canteen, which was in a building opposite the BBC. I think it was called The Langham. For the next two to three years I settled into a routine of going up to London once a month to record, usually four pieces at a time, but I had to be careful not to talk about the weather in the later recording. It seemed I went to a different studio every time, most of them in the main building, which I never realised before was built in the shape of a boat. One studio I went into was deep under the building. It was quite large and used for recording music. I was told it was so deep that sometimes the underground trains could be heard rumbling through underneath.

John Dunn had this lovely gentle voice which went with his personality. He was a truly gentle giant who made you feel at ease. I said to him once that a good interviewer is like a good doctor, he makes you feel at your ease. I remember having a conversation with him about being yourself when broadcasting. We came to the conclusion that it was probably impossible.

After about six months the programme had a new producer, Brian Willey, who took over from John Malloy. I was lucky because Brian was interested in his garden and he wanted me to carry on. Sometimes he would come up with a topic he would like me to talk about. I remember he had a pampas grass which was two different colours. One year I made a recording to be broadcast on Christmas Day. I don't know how many people thought I was in the studio.

I was surprised how far Radio 2 was heard. I had a card from listeners who were in Germany who had lived at one time at Harestock and been customers on the nursery. They said it was nice to hear my voice and it reminded them of their time here. I also had a lovely letter from Mary Spalding who had been leading lady in Die Fledermaus some 20 years before and said that hearing my voice brought back happy memories of her time in Winchester.

One day two of my old schoolmasters from Peter Symonds came into the greenhouse where I was working. They said *"Ah, our television and radio celebrity"*. I felt like saying to them *"That's not what you said to me at school!"*. One of them was always saying *"You'll never get on like your brother"*.

I was the man in the garden on the John Dunn Show for about three years. In 1979 a different producer took over from Brian Willey. He had new ideas about the programme and gardening tips wasn't one of them. I had contributed over 130 pieces and it had been a wonderful experience being part of the programme.

I had still been doing pieces now and again for South Today, but by 1979 Michael Harman had retired and a new editor had taken over. Don Osmond was still the deputy editor. Jenni Murray had joined Bruce to present the programme. One warm sunny day in April I had a phone call, could I do a piece that evening? I think they must have been sat in the studio and someone said *"It's a lovely day for gardening, let's have a garden on the roof. Ring Austen and get him to come down"*. When I arrived I had to get all my plants, baskets and containers up on to the roof some four storeys high. We got everything into the lift, which went up to the top floor. We then had to carry everything else up a narrow staircase on to the roof. They did get me a table and a green cloth to cover it. There was a wonderful view looking right down Southampton Water. What hadn't been thought of was that at ground level it was a lovely day with a gentle breeze, but on the roof the gentle breeze was quite a strong wind coming right up Southampton Water and blowing my plants nearly horizontal. The next disappointment I had was that I was to do the piece with Jenni Murray, not Bruce. I had done one piece with her before. She didn't want to use my notes, as Bruce had always done, and as she didn't know very much about plants and gardening the questions she asked weren't very relevant. I had the feeling while we were doing it that it just wasn't working out like it should have done. I think the new editor when he saw it must have thought *"This is a load of rubbish"*. That was the last piece I did for South Today.

One benefit I did get though, through being on South Today, was I was able to go to Chelsea Flower Show on Press Day, without the crowds. I still went up with Bruce after I finished on South Today.

It was a great experience being on television and radio and when I look back on it now it seems a bit like a dream. Without Bruce's help and encouragement I wouldn't have had the experience, for which I am very grateful. Having been on television and radio I got lots of requests to give talks on different aspects of gardening. I think I must have been to all of the WIs around Winchester and district, some of them twice. The most popular subject was the care of pot plants. At one I went to, which shall be nameless, I took some time telling them how to keep the geranium which they had been growing in the garden during the winter. One lady at the back of the room said *"All I does is wrap them up in newspaper and put them under the bed"!* I did get a request from the Hampshire WI asking me if I would like to go on their list of speakers. I am afraid I declined the invitation, as I didn't like the idea of travelling to distant parts of the county on dark winter nights. I only gave my talks during the winter as I couldn't spare the time during the summer months.

The gardening clubs liked me to talk more about the growing of plants. When I gave my talks I never used slides. I usually took plants and garden sundries and tried to make it as practical as possible. Margaret Lee, who was the editor of the parish magazine, asked me if I would contribute a gardening piece. We agreed to call it 'Gardening Tips and Tales'. In every issue, as well as the growing tips, I included a verse of poetry or prose which I felt might be relevant. After a while I think readers were interested in looking out for the verse as much as the garden, so I thought I would include some of them among my recollections.

I'd rather be a "could be",
If I could not be an "are",
For a "could be" is a "may be"
With a chance of reaching far.
I'd rather be a "has been"
Than a "might have been" by far,
For a "might have been" has never been
But a "has" was once an "are".
Anon

Connie and myself in H.M.S Pinafore, Connie's first show after she had been ill

With Bruce Parker and Jenni Murray preparing to record a piece about roof gardens on the top of BBC South studio centre in Southampton

At Chelsea Flower Show talking to Harry Dodson who was the gardener in the BBC series the Victorian Garden

BBC

BRITISH BROADCASTING CORPORATION
SOUTHAMPTON STUDIO CENTRE
SOUTH WESTERN HOUSE SOUTHAMPTON S09 1PF
TELEPHONE AND TELEGRAMS SOUTHAMPTON 26201

Ref: MH/MCB

15th September, 1975

Dear Austen,

    Just a line to thank you for a very good series of garden spots. We have watched you develop over the weeks into a very relaxed, professional broadcaster and your informal manner has made the series extremely pleasant viewing.

    I hope we shall be able to make use of your services in the future, from time to time, and that you enjoyed working with us as much as we enjoyed having you.

Yours sincerely,

(Michael Harman)
News Editor, South

Austen Hooker Esq.,
Hooker's Nurseries,
Littleton,
Nr. WINCHESTER, Hants

Tape 14
Clubs and Associations

John and myself carried on playing cricket at the YMCA ground at Weeke until 1959. In that time we had built up a very reasonable team. We had a couple of young lads joined us; Tony Sacree was the son of my friend Cecil Sacree who was in the Operatic. One evening he said his son had just left school and was keen on joining a cricket team and was looking for somewhere to play, so I invited him to come along and join us at Weeke. He proved to be one of the most natural batsmen I ever played with. He hadn't had a lot of coaching, but had most of the shots in the book and became one of our best batsmen, if not the best. He did actually have a trial for the County. The other young lad who joined us straight from school was to make his name in another sport. Les Elms had spotted him playing in the local park and asked him if he would be interested in playing with us. When he joined he didn't have any kit, so Les got him a pair of boots and John bought him a pair of white flannels. He was also very talented and was soon hitting the ball out of the ground. He also proved to be a very good wicket keeper. His name was Terry Paine, who went on to play football for Southampton. Ted Bates, who was the manager of Southampton, took him straight from the Winchester second team to the Saints first. Terry also played for England and was in the squad who went on to win the World Cup in 1966, although he didn't play in the final because of Alf Ramsey's decision not to play wingers. He had played in some of the previous rounds. The last time I saw Terry we sat watching the cricket at the old County ground.

We had several characters in the team. There was Gerry Smerdon, who had a very loud voice. When he was bowling if he appealed he could be heard in the next parish. Another character was our president, General Pratt. He was mayor of Winchester and he would get on the bus with his mayoral chain on and chat to everyone. He was also on the committee of the Hampshire County Cricket Club and would arrange matches with us with some of the young players on the

County staff. He lived just up the road from the ground where the new Sunrise Nursing Home now is. He was also on the committee for the local YMCA and when he died in 1958 we lost our representative and started to get new restrictions on the way the club should be run and by 1959 we were getting a bit fed up being told what we had to do. Fortunately for us football was no longer being played at Littleton, so we approached the Parish Council to see if it was possible to re-form the YMCA club as the old Littleton club and play as Littleton. The Parish Council were only too pleased for us to return and play again on the old pitch, so in 1960 Littleton once more had its own club. Only two or three players from the YMCA didn't transfer over, but we did get quite a few new members from the village, which included Gerald Goater, my cousin, Ron Fordham, George Mortimer, Peter Elms and John Tutt, all useful players. Richard was only 15 at the time, but was developing into a useful left-handed bat and wicket keeper. It took quite a lot of hard work to try to get the wicket ready for the first game of the season. It could be a bit lively. We used the old Atco mower which Eddie Grace got in working order. Eddie, who had played pre-war, had come to live in Littleton. Peggy, his wife, volunteered to help with the teas, a job which she did for many years. To mow the outfield we bought one section of a gang mower from the Pilgrims' School, where Eddie Grace was groundsman. To pull this we bought an old, nearly clapped out, car which lasted the season. We did get another one again the following year. After that the Parish Council took over the mowing of the field, which was done by the County Council. Richard did a lot of the mowing in the first two years. We used to say he learnt to drive mowing the rec. It was a good job there were no health and safety rules then.

Our new president was Mr. Lemon, the Chief Constable of Hampsire. He arranged for the groundsman from the County ground to pay us a visit and give us advice. As Mr. Lemon was our president our first game back at Littleton was against the Police. I had been captain for the last few years at the YMCA and continued with the job, one which I always enjoyed. I liked the tactics of the game. I also had the job of looking after the wicket. One year the groundsman from Sparsholt was playing against us and he asked me what I put on the wicket. I told him how I mixed my own fertiliser and spread it on. Unfortunately he mixed it up alright, but then spread it on with a shovel instead of gently spreading it on and burnt great swathes across their wicket. It was a good job he only did half of it. So they only had half a wicket to play on that season.

I had a friend, Roy Furmidge who was in charge of all the roads in the area. He was a supporter of Derbyshire Cricket Club and we were talking cricket one day and I was telling him about the work I was doing on the wicket. He said *"I'll get one of our chaps to come in and flatten it with a heavy road roller if you like"*. One Saturday morning the roller arrived. As it made its way up the field I wondered what I'd done. The back two wheels were going in about two inches further than the front roller. The old chap who was doing the job said *"Don't worry, I've done this before"*. He started at the top end of the pitch. He was absolutely right, within a short time it developed into a very reasonable wicket.

For the first summer we didn't have a pavilion and had to use the village hall. The old pre-war packing case pavilion had long gone. During the winter we discovered that Mr. Kimber, a farmer in Crawley, had an old wooden bungalow for sale. It was rather small, but it had been lived in at one time. It was built in sections and bolted together. We bought it and one of his men brought it over to Littleton on a tractor trailer. The club members put it back together and when we went out to bat we had to go through the front door.

Because we were now a village team we were able to enter the village knock-out. We didn't do particularly well in 1960, but in 1961 we won the trophy in great style, beating Twyford in the final by seven wickets. I think receiving the cup as captain of the club was the highlight of my cricketing days. We did win it again a few years later.

John Tutt, who was the local vet and a very keen member of the club, gave a cup to be competed for by Littleton and Crawley every year. Sparsholt joined later, making it a threesome.

Other than the 20 over knock-out, all the cricket we played was friendly matches against mostly other villages. There wasn't any weekend league. Saturdays and Sundays we usually started at about 2.30 p. m. One team would bat until tea, at about 5 o'clock, and if they weren't all out, would declare. The other side would then endeavour to get the runs by 7.30 p. m. It sometimes finished in a draw, when many of the players would retire to the local hostelry.

In late September, usually the last game of the season, for many years we played an all day game against the Old Symondians. We would start about 11. 30 a. m. and stop for lunch at about 1 o'clock. This was always a large salad meal and sweet made by Mrs. Grace, helped by Connie and some other ladies. Time was taken over the meal and no-one seemed to be in a hurry to get back to the cricket. At about 2 p.m. the fielding side would stroll out onto the field and cricket would resume. About 4 o'clock play would stop once more and everyone would return to the village hall for tea, which again would not be hurried over before play was resumed. Play would finish at about 6.30 p.m. By that time the light would be fading as the evenings would be getting in. Everyone would return home feeling we had had a great day to finish the season. I think the old boys enjoyed it as much as we did. The result – I don't think that mattered.

I had always enjoyed being captain, but after about 10 years in the job I thought it was time to hand it over to someone else. At the AGM I was given one of the best back-handed compliments I ever had. I said to a friend that I thought so and so would make a good captain. He said "No, we want you to carry on, we don't want old so and so, he's too nice a chap". I did know what he meant. Being captain you very often have to make unpopular decisions, especially when picking the team.

Over the many years I played cricket it became so much part of my life that I thought the day would never come when I wouldn't play, but when they started to try and hide me in the field (I always prided myself on being a reasonable fielder) I realised it was time to hang up my bat. I look back on wonderful memories of days on the cricket field, although perhaps not quite so good when sat in the pavilion waiting for the rain to stop! I can understand why it was considered important as a character builder at school. You might get 50 one day and take five wickets, but the next week you could be out for a duck and hit all round the ground, not taking a wicket.

We all had our favourite ground. I think mine was the old Twyford ground up on the hill behind the village. I always seemed to get runs there. The last game I played there I managed 65 not out. I was batting with Eddie Grace, who had played before the war and it was the last game he played for the club. Appropriately he finished not out.

One day I remember for another reason. We were playing at Fleming Park, Eastleigh. I opened the batting with Brian Barfoot and was out first ball. The next man in was my young brother Richard. When we stopped for tea our score was 120 for 1. I was the 1. Both Brian and Richard had 50, Richard's first for the club. One of their bowlers said that the ball that bowled me was the only one that moved all the afternoon. Some consolation! We did however go on and win the match. I made many friends playing against different teams year after year. Most teams seemed to have brothers playing in them. There were the Collins at Sparsholt, the Rogers at Owslebury, the Maskell brothers at the Worthys. I now play bowls against Laddie Maskell. We have been playing sport against each other most of our lives. We started playing cricket and football when we were still at school and now, in our 80s, we are still competing at bowls. I tell him he's been a thorn in my side in sport all my life!

John carried on playing for a few more years, just making up the numbers. I couldn't do that, I had to take a full part or nothing. John eventually became the club president. About the time I gave up Andrew and Nigel started playing in the men's team. Richard was still in the team, so the family was well represented.

When we started playing again at Littleton in 1960, the cricket pitch and fields were the only part of the recreation ground being mown. The portion below the pitch was uneven with rough grass. Above the pitch, between the tennis courts and the cricket were the abandoned trenches and old allotments where brambles and bushes grew around them. The children's swings and see-saw were situated in the top right hand corner of the rec., next to the tennis courts. On the Parish Council we felt this was far from ideal, being hidden by the brambles and bushes. George Wadsworth, our chairman, said he would enquire of Ray Furmidge, our local County Council roads and bridges officer, if he could assist us in any way to clear the brambles and bushes. A few weeks later we had been out for the day and when we came back I looked up the recreation ground and wondered what had happened. All the brambles and bushes had disappeared. When I looked a bit closer I realised they had been completely pulverised. All that was left was shreds of wood and bushes cut into very tiny pieces. This was the first time I had ever seen the effects of a flail mower. We then had the site levelled and seeded with grass and shortly after this we followed by levelling the bottom half of the field.

The Council had a request to start the football again. To do this the Council had the whole of the rec. mown regularly by the County Council. Football was then played below the cricket square by the adult team, with a pitch for the junior team above the square.

In the village at the top of the hill, at the cross-roads opposite Deane Down Drove, is the field where the Bronze Age disc barrow is situated. This was known as the old recreation ground and was owned and run by the Parish Council. Between the wars it was grazed by a pony owned by Mr. Ward who lived in Deane Down Drove. When he gave up during the war a gentleman who lived in The Retreat in Main Road used it to tether his goats. After the war no-one wanted to use it anymore. It was no use for sport of any kind, the only use was for people to exercise their dogs. It just got left. Only the disc barrow and a smaller bowlbarrow near it were kept clear. By 1960 the rest of the field had reverted from downland into being covered by thorn bushes. The field was a liability to the Parish Council and the question came up on council as to what could be done with it. The idea was put forward – why not use some of it for building. As it was a site of historical interest permission to sell it had to be obtained from the appropriate authority. There were several ideas as to how it could be laid out. I remember one grand idea was to have the disc barrow in the middle with a road and houses round it. Eventually the Council was given permission to sell two plots of land near the road. The money obtained could only be used for recreational purposes in the village, but only three-quarters of it, the other quarter was to be reinvested and the interest, when it had reached the original full amount, could then be used and then the whole process repeated. The sale of the two plots took place in a hotel in Winchester. The estimated price it was expected to fetch was around £12,000. Most of the members of the Council were at the sale and I remember our excitement when the first plot went for £8,500 and the second went for £9,000, a total of £17,500. This money gave sport in Littleton a real boost. With additional grants which came from the Playing Fields Association the pavilion was built, two new hard tennis courts were made and the bowling green was put in. All have been a great success and thrive.

One of the players in the village cricket team at that time was Vic Lewis whose son was a professional cricketer playing for Hampshire County Cricket Club. Together they organised a team from the County to play Littleton team to celebrate the official opening of the pavilion. The date was 25 April. There were quite a number of the first team players in the Hampshire side. Unfortunately it didn't just rain, it snowed! The official opening took place in the pavilion and the two teams played one another at table tennis in the village hall.

In 1967 George Wadsworth had retired as chairman of the Parish Council and his place was taken by Harold Mason, who had overseen the building of the pavilion, the tennis courts and the bowling green. The new courts had been opened by Bruce Parker, South Today presenter, who at that time lived in the parish on Harestock Road.

In late 1972 a meeting was held with the idea of forming a bowling club. This was agreed and the club was to be known as the Littleton Bowling Club. The subscription for 1972/73 was fixed at 50p. Dad was a member of the committee. I purposely didn't want to get too involved as I was still helping to prepare the wicket for the cricket club. The first newsletter of the bowling club said there was to be a new bowling green created on the recreation ground and that the green was to be screened, fenced and seeded. The green was constructed by a company from Chandlers Ford in 1973. Because it was seeded and not turfed, they insisted on calling it a bowling lawn. A lot of work had to be done voluntarily by members before it was fit to start play in 1975. The most laborious job was picking up the stones. I tried not to get too involved. I did help in an advisory capacity. One of the main helpers in the maintenance team was Alf Faulkner.

In the very early days some of the committee meetings were held in the office of our garden centre. The green gradually began to improve, but it must have been five or six years before it could really be called a bowling green. Membership of the club grew quickly and fixtures with most of the clubs around were arranged. The club also entered a couple of leagues. For many years I enjoyed playing in the Whitchurch league. One year four members of the club won the county fours. We also had club competitions. I played in the triples with Anne and Ray Wiggle and the mixed pairs with Anne, with a reasonable amount of success over the years.

In the early 1980s I started playing in the winter. This was held at the Sports Centre in Winchester. We played on a mat laid on a sports surface. In 1990 I started playing with Anne and Ray at the proper indoor green at Whitchurch. In 1997 a new indoor green was opened in Winchester next to the Sports Centre. I have been playing there every Friday in the winter with Anne and Ray, again with a reasonable amount of success and a lot of enjoyment.

In the 1970s the Parish Council formed what is known as the Activities Committee. It was to be independent of the Parish Council. The first thing that it did was to form a Senior Citizens' Club. It was run to start with by younger people, but after a short time the senior citizens took it over and ran it themselves. Dad was on the committee and took on the job of treasurer when he was 90! They met regularly in the village hall and also went out during the summer on coach trips, but the main event was their Christmas meal and party, where I regularly used to help with the entertainment.

Harold Mason had taken part in the two flower shows we held in 1956 and 1957 and was keen to see if we could revive it. A decision was made by the Activities Committee to stage a show in the village hall in 1971. A fete was also held in the recreation ground to raise funds to support the show. The WI served tea and refreshments in an old army tent just outside the kitchen door. The show was well supported with over 250 entries. Everyone agreed it was a great success, even the WI ladies serving the tea, in spite of being pestered by wasps. For a second show the main committee was divided into two sub-committees, one to organise the fete and the other to run the flower show, each had their own secretary. The flower show secretary was Ted Wedge, a job he did for many years. Ted was the village policeman. Connie and myself were both on the flower show sub-committee. It was decided that in 1972 we would have a small marquee for the exhibits and the WI would use the hall for teas. This has been the format ever since.

It was decided right from the start that the main purpose of the show was to be a day for the village when everyone could meet up for a relaxing day of fun and the flower show. The show went from strength to strength, getting larger every year with different items being added. There was a carnival procession winding its way to the ground from the Henry Beaufort School and a horse show added after a few years. This got so popular that we just didn't have the room and it is now held a week before the show at Headbourne Worthy. At that time we didn't have the extension to the recreation ground that we have now. All we had was the six acres of the old recreation ground and parking cars became a real problem. When the Council bought the Jubilee field next to the ground in 1977 it helped the show problem with car parking.

Being on the show committee means a lot of work, but we all enjoyed it. There was always the worry of whether people would enter. They would leave putting in their entries until the very last minute – 6. 00 p.m. on the Wednesday before the show. We were always relieved when we knew the number of entries. The part of the show I've always enjoyed the most is the morning, when everyone is arriving with their exhibits, full of expectation. The smell in the marquee of the flowers and vegetables mixed with the smell of the grass underfoot brings back the memories of my childhood. I have exhibited every year since 1971. I always enjoy meeting with old friends who I only see once a year. George Lowe from Sparsholt, who has competed since 1972, is a real old professional gardener and we always have plenty of comparisons to make. The show must now be one of the largest village shows in Hampshire. It has become one day of the year when all the village meets and brings people from all walks of life together. The flower show has been a village tradition for nearly 100 years and it still has the atmosphere and ability to bring villagers together as it did in those early days. I hope the youngsters of today remember it as I did as a child and will make sure it continues for many years to come.

In 1987 a gardening club was formed as part of the horticultural section of the show. Ray Broughton, a lecturer in the horticultural department at Sparsholt College, had come to live in South Drive in the village. He immediately became involved in the show and, together with Ted Wedge, a meeting was held in the church room to launch the club. So many people turned up it was a job to fit everyone in. Ray became chairman, Ted Wedge secretary and Norman Cox was treasurer. He was already treasurer of the show. Meetings were held every third Wednesday in the month and still are. After about three years the club broke away from the show and became a club in its own right and managed its own finances. Over the years membership has grown from about 40 to about 100. Dorothy Highfield is now the chairman and Barbara Elsmore the secretary. Ray Broughton is now the president and still gives an entertaining lecture once a year. I have been on the committee right from the start and was president for a few years and am now a patron.

By 1972 I had been on the Parish Council for 12 years and felt it was time to stand down and make way for someone else to take part in village affairs. It had been 12 very busy years. Harestock estate, which is part of the parish, had been developed and my job was to make sure that the path which ran along the parish boundary between Harestock and Weeke was kept open by developers. The Memorial Hall was given a complete renovation. The recreation ground was cleared and levelled so that we had two football pitches and cricket ground. A new children's playground was put in. Part of the old recreation ground was sold and the money used for a new pavilion and bowling green and two hard courts added to the two grass. On Harestock estate land was bought for a children's playground. It must have been one of the busiest times the Parish Council ever had.

Zerpose oi must out wi' the mowing machine
An' water the grass for ter meake of it grean,
Vor today they be playin' at cricket:
An' chop down they nettles as grow by yon wall
Or they'll waste 'alf o' match a-zeeking the ball
When it's gorn away off o' the wicket.

Come, give oi a 'and with yon roller, my zon,
Though oi reckon it robs the wold Geame ov its vun
To smooth out they bumps on the wicket.
Now, when oi were a youngster oi used vor to learn
Which 'ummock to 'it vor to meake the ball turn
Too sharp for 'em even to flick it.

Robert Dalzell Dillon Thomas

YMCA cricket team 1956. Back row from left: A Nicholls, G Smerdon, P Eldridge, W Alexander, G Strange, B Barfoot, C Emery, M Wright, K Guppy. Middle row: W Snow, L Elms, A Smith, A Hooker, J Rickman Front: T Paine, J Hooker

Littleton winners of the village knock-out 1961. Back row from left: Umpire, J Hooker, B Barfoot, L Elms, K Guppy, C Warwick, A Hooker, P Beckwith, P Durrant. Front: R Hooker, A Nicholls, G Goater, T Sacree

Receiving the cup from the chairman of the Winchester district council. A proud moment

The sports pavilion built with the help of money raised by the sale of two plots of land on the old recreation ground. The money was also used to build two new hard tennis courts and a bowling green

Enjoying a game of bowls

The flower show now one of the largest village shows in Hampshire

With Ted Wedge admiring the onions. Ted was not only village policeman he was secretary of the show and gardening club, ran the youth club and taught the youngsters cycling safety, captain of the cricket team, sacristan in St Catherine's church and was in the miz-maze folk dance team

Members of the gardening club and WI prepare for the plant sale May 2005

Tape 15
The Community

In 1981 Geoff Allen had an idea which originated the previous year in his garage of an evening of nostalgia called 'Eve of Eve' and held in the village on 23rd December. The hall was decorated like a drawing room of days gone by. It started with the arrival of the carol singers. This was followed by entertainment with different adults and children doing their party piece, in the way the family would have done in the days before radio and television. These would be interspersed with carols sung by the choir and the audience. Geoff would sit in his chair by the fireplace and compere the evening. The entertainment would consist of Christmas readings, songs and instrumentalists. The children would act out a little play, often about Christmas Eve and Father Christmas. The evening would draw to a close with a made-up pantomime, with the men taking all the parts, many forgetting their words and making them up, which added to the hilarity. The boar's head carol would be sung and the boar's head would for many years be carried in by Ted Wedge, the village policeman. The evening would end with Patrick bringing in the figgy pudding. I am pleased to say this event is still carried on. It is never advertised, but is always packed out.

In 1987, because of the new fire regulations brought in and the number allowed in the hall, this event was moved to Crawley village hall. A few years after this I was talking to Geoff and said *"what we need in Littleton is a new hall"* and Geoff said *"That would be a good job for Clive Thompsett when he retires"*. One day in the spring of 1994 I was working on the nursery when Barbara Kingston came in to see me. She said she was representing the Parish Council and they were considering the future of the village hall and wished to form a working party to do a feasibility study on the options. Whether it could be modified, improved or replaced. So she asked me if I would be willing to be on the working party. When I replied that I would be only too pleased to help, I think she was a little surprised, thinking because of my long association with the old hall I might have been against any proposal to replace it. The working party came to the conclusion that the only real option was to build a new hall on an adjacent site. A public meeting was held in February 1995. The old hall was packed with 120 people. The decision to build a new hall was passed, with 114 in favour and six abstentions. A fundraising committee was formed, with 30 volunteers. Six trustees were elected, with Clive Thompsett chairman, Barbara Kingston secretary, Ernest Witts treasurer, together with Geoff Allen, Mike Farrell and myself.

Shortly after the public meeting the Millennium section of the Lottery was announced and in late April 1995 the trustees presented an application for a grant. In July they were informed that the request for a grant had been turned down on the grounds that the building was insufficiently distinctive. The trustees, with the help of the architect and a more distinctive building, which also included a sculpture, submitted a second application to the Millennium Commission in February 1996. On this occasion they were successful.

Several other grants were obtained, from the Parish Council; Hampshire County Council; Winchester City Council and the Pike Trust. In the five years up to the opening of the hall, the fundraising committee held over 150 events. I remember Clive saying when we started the project that we were going to raise the money and enjoy doing it. We certainly did. We held such a wide range of events, too many to mention. A bi-monthly newsletter was distributed to keep parishioners up to date with the events programme and progress so far.

Building started in July 1998 and it was handed over to the trustees in February 1999. A very nice de-commissioning ceremony was held in March, when the memorials were removed from the old hall and placed in the specially built recess in the foyer of the new. They were carried by members of the Parish Council, with a guard of honour and accompanied by the 'Last Post' played by the buglers of the Light Division. When the memorials were in place in the new hall, a bugler played reveille. While all this was taking place I kept thinking how much Dad and Grandad would have approved. I am sure they would have felt, like I did, that the soul of the old hall was passing over to the new. The following week the old hall was demolished. I had very divided feelings when they started to take it apart. I had spent some of the happiest times of my life in the old building. When I saw the floorboards being taken away on a lorry I remembered what Grandad said when the old hall was being built – they had to be laid three times before they were satisfied. I also remember the time we polished them so hard with candlewax for ballroom dancing classes it turned out more like a skating rink and made it difficult for the dancers to stand up! Perhaps it was a lucky omen that the floorboards in the new hall also had to be taken up and re-laid. I feel sure I am speaking for all those who had many happy times in the old hall as I did, that we were grateful for the foresight our predecessors had in building it.

As we lived next to the new hall, Connie and myself kept a photographic record of the hall being built. Every time we heard a lorry arrive we would rush out and take a photo. It might be the bricks arriving or perhaps the new chairs. We also kept a photographic record of most of the fundraising events which were held over the five years. On 15th May 1999 a large crowd, including five ladies who had been at the opening of the old hall, assembled for the official opening ceremony. This was carried out by Mr. James Butler, Deputy Lieutenant of Hampshire, and was dedicated by our new rector, Rev. Juliet Montague. The five ladies who had been present at the opening of the old hall were presented with a bouquet by five children who were born at the same time as the decision to build a new hall was made. After the opening, afternoon tea was available, children were entertained by a clown and Punch and Judy, and children's races. In the hall an exhibition of different activities by village groups was on show. The band of the Light Division from the Sir John Moore Barracks played for the ceremony. During the evening the centre of the recreation ground was cleared and the band and bugles of the Light Division sounded the retreat with a display of marching. Another attraction was a whole pig roast. The Twin Rivers jazz band played under the veranda with dancing on the grass round the sculpture.

Some of the events were mirrored on the opening of the old hall. I feel sure that if any of those involved in building the old hall could have been there they would have been just as proud of what had been achieved as we were. Of all the different happenings and events and projects I have been involved with during my lifetime in the village, being involved with the building of the Millennium Memorial Hall comes top of the list. There was something about the whole atmosphere it created in bringing the parish together with a meeting of people. I know I met and made many new friends who I would not have known otherwise. Because of the way the whole project was carried out there is a real feeling of achievement and pride among the parish folk in their village hall. We are also pleased that most of the things which were given so much thought, time and planning have worked out so well. Now, ten years on, it is very rare to walk around the rec. and not see the hall in use.

During my life in the village, the two centres of the community have been the village hall and recreation ground and St. Catherine's Church. By the church, I mean the people. For 50 years since the Rev. Earle was incumbent the church has had an active influence in village life. When the Rev. Bell left for pastures new, he was followed by the Rev. Hogg who was a bachelor, but unfortunately he only stayed for about 18 months before leaving to take up a post in South Africa. We were rather sorry to lose him. He was keen on playing squash and would call in for David to play with him at the Lido in Winchester. The following rector was the Rev. Richard Johnson. He was also a bachelor. He moved into the new rectory built in the Glebe field next to the church room, so our new rector now lived in Littleton instead of Crawley. His mother, who lived to be 100, lived with him. While he was incumbent, the parish of Sparsholt was amalgamated with Littleton and Crawley, so that he had three parishes to look after.

Richard very often came into the nursery, he liked having a chat with Dad, they had both spent time in India. Richard was very good with the older generation and was keen on the senior citizens' club. He came in one day and said he had been given by Miss Edmunds some old glass slides of the village which had been taken mostly between the wars by her uncle, Rev. Tanner. He also said Mrs. Lionel Deane would like to see them and he had fixed an evening at her house to show them. He had borrowed an old projector, or magic lantern, to show them and would I like to join them. When I arrived at Mrs. Deane's he had fixed up the old lantern with a hairdryer attached to keep it cool, a bit of a Heath Robinson affair. The slides were the same ones the Rev. Tanner had shown to the church fellowship some 25 years before. Unfortunately several of the slides were dropped and broken during the evening, so it was decided then and there to have them transferred into slides which could be used in an up-to-date projector.

Another idea was put forward. Why not have an evening in the church room when they could be shown to people in the village who might be interested? From the meeting, the Littleton Local History Group was formed. The group have nearly always met in the church room, where we had many interesting speakers. We have had trips out to many interesting places, including visits to other villages and finding out about their history. We have not done any real excavations, but have been field walking, where we found a lot of ancient pottery. In 1985 the History Group started a project where we recorded everything that went on in the village during the year, called the 'Chronicling of Littleton'. It was an idea put forward by our secretary, Philip Lloyd. Most of it comprised written or photographs of all the main events taking place in the village. It also recorded personal items, like where people went for a drink or a meal. It also included personal costs etc. This was put into a sealed envelope not to be opened for 50 years. Two or three professional photographers took many photographs of different parts and events in the parish. Connie made a scrapbook of press cuttings, programmes and service sheets. At the end of the year the whole project was collated together and put into the Hampshire County archives.

In 1987 the History Group entered the project in a competition run by the Hampshire Magazine entitled 'Village Ventures'. The group was successful in winning the miscellaneous section. There were five different categories in the competition. We didn't win the overall prize, but we were given very high praise by the judges. The report of the presentation in the press reads -

"Chronicling Littleton in 1985 by the Local History Group won the written and miscellaneous section of the competition. This was a unique undertaking in national terms and has never been attempted before. The object was to chronicle through the means of the written word, photographs, videotape and film the life of the village of Littleton during the year 1985. Major events in the village, the flora, the fauna, even the activities of worms during this period were listed. Among the most fascinating were the details of people's daily lives, where they shopped, where they worshipped, whether they went out for a meal or a drink and their attitudes to life in the parish as well as the hobbies, sports and crafts they took part in. The idea was inspired by the 900th anniversary of Doomsday and it is difficult to imagine a better way of celebrating the event with such lasting value to future historians and an endless fascination to locals in years to come."

At the end of all the presentations the judge had this to say :

"A special mention must be made of the originality of the work of the Littleton Local History Group. If it were possible to produce a special prize in addition, the Littleton Local History Group would receive it. This is an imaginative and positive project that not only Littleton can feel proud of, but Hampshire and, indeed, the nation."

The presentation took place at Bishops Waltham and, as Philip Lloyd was unable to attend, I had the honour of accompanying Richard Johnson, our chairman, when he received the award together with a cheque for £100. Littleton also won second prize in the environmental section of the competition for work involving the improvement of the village pond.

The latest project accomplished by the group has been to publish a book entitled "Littleton 1900 – 2000". This took some three years to put together by members under the editorship of Mike Lupton.

One evening in March 1974 I had just arrived at the opera rehearsal in St. Maurice's hall in Winchester when one of the members who lived in Crawley said she had just passed Littleton Church which was on fire. The fire did considerable damage. It destroyed the organ and did a certain amount of damage to the roof over the north aisle. The rest of the church also had a lot of smoke damage. The old organ was no great loss, it was in a very poor state. I can remember Uncle Fred, who had been church organist twice, once after the First World War and during the Second in the 1940s, getting annoyed about the bad state it was in, saying that it wanted scrapping. The fire happened during the interregnum between Rev. Hogg leaving and before the new incumbent, Rev. Richard Johnson, was inducted in May, and as the new rectory had not been finished he arrived without a church or a rectory and he had to hold his first service in the church room. Richard Johnson retired in 1990 and went to live in South Wonston with his mother.

We hadn't had a young rector in Littleton for some years until David Williams came in 1990 to live in the rectory with his wife Jo and their young family. He was very popular, especially with the youngsters and was also keen on sport and walking. The congregation was growing so large it was becoming difficult to get everyone into our little church on special occasions. The decision was made to reinstate the gallery, which had once been in the church and was moved during the restoration in the late 1800s. The cost was £24,000, the total amount being raised in one weekend. The gallery was built with the oak which had been blown down in the gale of 1987. In 1997 David moved on to take up the post of rector at St. Mary's, Andover. There was a gap of two years before our new rector arrived. Tim Maguire and John Cranmer, who was a resident of Crawley, did a great job holding the fort during the interregnum. In March 1999 Littleton had its first female rector, Juliet Montague, her husband Fred and her mother and father came to live in the rectory. After her induction in Crawley at a reception in the village hall, one of the parishioners of her previous parish who had come a long way to see her inducted, said to me *"You have pinched our rector"*, to which I replied *"Someone else pinched ours!"*. I felt Juliet must have been held in high regard for someone to come so far for her induction and to make that remark.

One of Juliet's first jobs in the village was the dedication and opening of the new hall. A difficult situation she had to deal with was when Kevin Lay, our church warden, was killed in a plane crash in Kosovo. He had volunteered to help Tear Fund in the re-building of the homes of the ethnic Albanians. Kevin was a member of the Tear Fund disaster response team. I had known Kevin since he was a little boy when he would sometimes come on the nursery with his older brother David and play with David, Andrew and Nigel. Like all of us younger brothers, he was very keen to keep up with his older sibling. He always seemed to have a happy, cheeky face. When he went to Henry Beaufort School, John would pick him up and take him when he took Nigel and Andrew. In their later days at Henry Beaufort Kevin didn't want a lift, he had found a young lady to escort to and from school. This was Lyn, who was later to become his wife. As a man, Kevin still had his cheerful smile and was always ready to help anyone. I am sure many of us can remember an occasion when he was there when needed. Kevin's death had a profound impact on those of us in the village who knew him. Here was a man who was killed going to another country to help others in a dire situation. I'm sure many of us were asking questions to which we found it difficult to find an answer. A service of thanksgiving was held in St. Catherine's Church on a cold November day. The church was full to overflowing. Many of us took part in the service in a marquee outside to which the service was relayed. A trust fund in memory of Kevin was set up, which is known as the Kevin Lay Foundation, to help other young people carry on the work he had been doing by helping others less fortunate.

The benefice of Littleton, Crawley and Sparsholt has now been amalgamated with Wherwell and Chilbolton. Juliet has a large area to cover with the help of three curates and three readers. I suppose in my lifetime the biggest change in the church has been the ordination of women. Juliet has shown that this calling can be carried out by a woman just as well as by any man. I believe that the ordination of women has been the best thing that has happened to the church in my lifetime.

Although the church building is situated at one end of the village, the church people have been at the centre of village life for the past 50 years and have had a large part to play in the community spirit which has prevailed. It is the people, not the church building, which make the church and this is certainly the case in Littleton. Perhaps because of my feeling that the church should be part of village life, I remember as a teenager the Rev. Thornley saying to me one day when he came on to the nursery *"I haven't seen you in church lately"*. I so wanted to say to him *"I haven't seen you in the village lately"*. We boys had a club and he was always going to visit us, but he never did. I know he was an old man at the time, but it was about ten years later when I asked him if he would publish my bans of marriage. As I have already said, he said *"Austen, nothing would give me greater pleasure"*. Unfortunately he read the first time, but was too ill to call the second or third, which was called by Mr. Pitney. Rev. Thornley was over 80 by that time and was forced to retire because of ill health. I don't think he would have been allowed to carry on so long today. It is comforting to know that the church in the village is thriving as much now, if not more than it has ever done.

Stand still and look, and see with awe
What twice ten thousand fingers wrought
And find in each and every Village Hall
Gifts priceless that no purchase bought.

Written by Karl Shawler
about the WI in 1955

As Buttons in the Eve of Eve pantomime

Fundraising – David, Margaret and myself 'the Hooker Team' taking part in the sponsored swim

Trustees on site selecting bricks for the new hall. Myself, Barbara Kingston, Ernest Witts, Geoff Allen, Clive Thompsett and Linda Brown, architect

The first topsoil being removed

The memorial together with the roll of honour being transferred from the old to the new led by Rev Tim Maguire and carried by members of the parish council. The soul of the old hall passing to the new

The new Millennium Memorial Hall

Tape 16
Conclusions

My favourite author is the countryman farmer and broadcaster A. G. Street. His descriptive writing about the countryside is second to none. He was very often called "the Cobbett of our time" and his great friend and colleague Macdonald Hastings thought he was even better. I especially like his description of the first signs of spring. How he walks up the lane describing everything going on around him with the words "It was all warm and February". The one day you get that tells you that spring is just around the corner. I have collected all his books and have had great fun in visiting nearly every second-hand bookshop I came across. Most of them are now first edition, with one or two autographed. I also have his daughter Pam Street's book on her father's life. My desert island book would have to be Macdonald Hastings' country book, an anthology of rural writing. It does include some pieces by A. G. Street.

Over the years Mum suffered periods of depression and spent time in and out of different hospitals. She did have times when she was a little better and she would work in the shop where she had her special customers. In 1985 Mum and Dad celebrated their Diamond Wedding, with a telegram from the Queen, which Mum liked. Unfortunately, after the celebration Mum was not so good again and in January 1986 she went into Cornerways in Kings Worthy for a fortnight, just to give Dad and Anne a bit of a break. One evening she was just sat watching television when she passed away. Really a wonderful way to go, sat holding the hand of a friend. Her funeral was held on a very mild January day, I remember Dad saying as we walked up the path to the cemetery, "Hark at the birds singing".

Dad was 89 when Mum died, but he was still quite active. He liked doing little jobs in the greenhouses, mainly taking cuttings. He grew a few vegetables in his garden, especially runner beans. He enjoyed the Senior Citizens' Club and took on the job of treasurer when he was 90. He also still liked his game of bowls, playing with his old friend Ernie Janes, who had been head stud groom at

Littleton Stud. They called themselves the Ancient Britains. He had been in hospital for a prostate operation when he was 87 and he would say *"look at that poor old chap over there"*, who was probably someone about 10 years younger than him. In the summer of 1990 Dad began to get a problem with his back and had trouble getting about. He was disappointed when he couldn't get to the Show in early September, but sat by the window of the old house and watched people come and go to the Show ground. His health gradually deteriorated over the next three weeks and he died in the early hours of 23rd September, the day after Anne's birthday. He did have a drop of sherry to wish her a happy day. Dad was one of the last of the real old nurserymen whose skills died with him. They didn't have things like thermostats or soil analysis and many other aids we have today. They had to use their experience and skill. Dad could walk into a greenhouse and tell what the temperature was within two degrees Fahrenheit and if you needed to put an extra one shovel of coal on the boiler or two. He could tell if a plant wanted watering or feeding just by looking at it. Dad also kept a diary and it was no good telling him that the weather was any different than it had ever been. Another thing he did, like many of the old gardeners, was to keep certain records on the greenhouse door. The two I remember were the date when he heard the first cuckoo in spring, the most usual date was 20th April, my birthday. Unfortunately we seldom hear the cuckoo today. The other record he kept was extremes of weather, such as the amount of snow and the lowest and highest temperatures.

All Dad ever wanted to be was a nurseryman and have his own nursery to grow his beloved flowers. He would spend every hour he could on the nursery. I remember Mum getting a bit fed up sometimes and she would say to him *"Why don't you take your bed down there?"*. He loved the Winchester Horticultural Society meetings where he would meet up with all his old gardening friends. In later years he would be picked up by his great friend, Bill Boyd, from Sparsholt College, and taken to the meetings. He also enjoyed going with several of them to other horticultural societies on gardening quizzes and panels.

During the few weeks before he died we would sit up with him at night. They were some precious moments. He would talk about times past, especially concerning his early days in Littleton. He also talked about his experiences in the First World War, things he had never talked about before. One night he *said "I never even told Mum this."* 'It was in August 1918 towards the end of the war and they were advancing across a cornfield when the Germans started shelling them. He threw himself on the ground and there was a blinding flash. When he came round he looked down and couldn't see his legs and thought *"My God, I've lost my legs"*. He then tried to see if he could move and feel for them. He managed to pull one out of the ground. He then felt for the other leg and managed to pull that out and when he looked around he was actually in the shell hole and he didn't have a scratch, but the man next to him had completely disappeared, only his tin hat was left. Dad stood up, picked up the other chap's tin hat because he had lost his own, and went on across the field.

Dad had a very placid temperament and I can't ever remember him losing his temper. He also had a wonderful sense of humour with the ability to laugh at himself. He loved "Dad's Army" on the television; he said it was just like that. All his friends and associates from the village and horticulture gathered at the village church for his funeral to the sound of his signature tune, the Intermezzo from Cavalleria Rusticana. After a little bit of persuasion, Richard Johnson came back for the funeral and gave the address, one of the best I ever heard Richard give. He hadn't wanted to tread on the toes of our new rector, David Williams, but he came when he knew it was David's idea.

It often seems in a family that everything sails along with nothing happening, and then suddenly everything happens at once. Marriages, births and deaths. This happened to our family in the years between 1986 and 1996. In 1985 John's son Nigel had a very serious brain operation, which he recovered from. In the autumn of 1990 he married Wendy and the following spring their son Jack was born. Unfortunately Nigel's illness returned and he was having problems with his balance. On 17th August 1991 Andrew was married to Nicky at St. Mary's Church, Pulborough. This was a really happy day with all their relations and friends. Several of the villagers made the trip down. Anne and Ray Wiggle and Margaret Lee called in on their way back from holiday in Sussex. There were also six or seven of Andrew's veterinary colleagues and many of Nicky's friends and family. The reception was held in the Old Barn in Slinfold. By the time of Andrew's wedding Nigel's condition had worsened considerably, but he was determined to get to the wedding. They had always been great pals as boys, spending hours on the rec. playing cricket. During the rest of the summer Nigel's condition gradually got worse. When he died on 31st October it was a great shock to all the family and it was a real hammer blow to John. They had been more than father and son; they were great mates, with their love of cricket, trains and the countryside.

On 25th April 1993 we celebrated our Ruby Wedding with a party in the village hall. It was a very happy occasion, with David supplying his disco for young and old to dance to. The best present that day was when Andrew and Nicky told us we were going to be grandparents. Kate was born on 28th December in hospital in Yeovil. The following day we drove down in the pouring rain to see her and Nicky. I can still remember the wonderful feeling when I held her for the first time. It was one of those in depth feelings which are indescribable and unique and as I write this she has just celebrated her 16th birthday and is a lovely young lady.

David and Jackie were married on 11th June 1994, followed by a blessing in St. Catherine's Church given by the rector, David Williams. The reception was held at the Game Larder, Stockbridge. This was followed by a disco held in the Civil Service Club on Flowerdown. A very busy and happy day. We now had two sons, two daughters and one granddaughter, soon to be followed by a second granddaughter, Samantha, born to Andrew and Nicky on 5th January 1996 at Dorchester Hospital. She has beaten me into print, having just had a little story which she has written published in a book called "Young Writers' Mini Sagas". The story had to be no more than 50 words. There is something wonderful about grandchildren, perhaps all the joy without the responsibilities.

In 1993 John was 67 and I was 65 and we spent a lot of our time working, especially during the bedding season when it was virtually a seven day week. Our thoughts turned to how we might retire. The field next door to the nursery had just been developed, with some quite large houses. We decided to explore the possibility of developing the nursery, but were turned down with some very extraordinary reasons. One was we were extending into the countryside. We were in fact in the middle of the village and they had built on the field next door. Another reason was that the roofs of the houses would be seen from the recreation ground. We appealed against the refusal and our appeal was upheld, with the Inspector being quite scathing against the City Council planner. One thing he did say was *"In no way can you say this is extending into the countryside"* and that the recreation ground is a large area and roofs of houses can already be seen from many parts. With the appeal upheld we were able to approach the developers and were successful in selling an option to Clarks the developers. As a safeguard this had a time limit of about three years.

On Easter weekend 1996 it was my turn to be on duty and John's weekend off. Saturday lunchtime John went off with the words *"See you on Monday"*. Sunday afternoon Betty, John's wife, rang to say John had been taken into hospital with a suspected heart attack. She had been in to see him and was going back later. As it was Easter Sunday and I had been working all day, I went to Evensong at St. Catherine's. When I came out Richard's van was pulled up by the church gate. I knew something must be wrong and then Richard told me the sad news. John had had a second heart attack and not come round. The loss of John hit me more than anything I had experienced before. We were always close, having been brought up together and worked together. The only time we were apart was the two years when he was in the Army.

Everyone liked John; he always had the same placid temperament. He never seemed to have much luck in life. He was married twice and then he lost Nigel, something he never ever got over. I think had Nigel lived, John would still be alive. He really did die of a broken heart. One of his favourite sayings in life was *"Anything for a quiet life"*. Unfortunately it wasn't like that for John. John's relationship with his customers was shown by their response when he died. We were always making wreathes etc. for the gypsy community and we had one gentleman who regularly came in to order them. A day or two after John died he came in to order a wreath. When we asked him who it was for, he replied *"For your brother, he has always been so helpful to me over the years"*.

The loss of John put an extra load on to Richard's and my shoulders and we now had to be on duty every other weekend. It also put extra pressure on the finances. I was now 68 and my thoughts again turned to being able to retire. Clarks had not taken up their option to buy the land and we were now able to put it back on the market. We eventually agreed a sale with Wates, again with a timescale. This gave us about a year to run down the business and we had a sale on 5th July 1997. I retired with very mixed feelings. I had spent all my life living on the nursery and it held so many happy memories. The sale was a bit of a heart rending day, seeing many of the old familiar items sold. It was not a very successful sale, most things going cheap, the only thing which did make a good price was the David Brown tractor which fetched nearly as much as we had paid for it 25 years before. As it turned out we needn't have been in such a hurry to have a sale, as Wates developers were not in a hurry to develop the site. The next two years turned out to be a nightmare. We were a bit like piggy in the middle, with the developers on one side and the planners on the other.

Because my bungalow was on the site it meant I had to find somewhere else to live. Through the WI Connie had met Bettine, who lived in Rozelle Close. Unfortunately she hadn't lived there long before she died. We didn't know her daughters or where they lived, so we put a note through the door of the bungalow saying we might be interested if they decided to sell. Two or three days later Anne, Bettine's daughter, rang us to say they were selling and invited us to view it. When we saw the bungalow we didn't have second thoughts, it was exactly what we were looking for. It is on the edge of the village looking across a pleasant garden towards the fields where horses grazed. Bettine had been keen on her garden. We agreed a price with Anne and her sister Jean, thinking it wouldn't be too long before we received the money for the nursery. Perhaps we were a little naive, not having dealt with developers before, and thinking they would get on with the job. After about six months there was still no progress, but Anne and Jean were very patient. After another three months they said they felt they would have to put it on the market and I couldn't blame them, but there was really nothing I could do. I think they did get an offer for the bungalow, but after a time that fell through. Anne rang me and said they would still accept my offer. After about another three months it was still dragging on. We did know that Wates would have to finalise by October or lose the deposit. After talking it over with Anne and Jean I agreed to pay them a temporary rent, to be paid once a month. When we closed the nursery for the first time in my life I didn't have a garden, so I took on an allotment in Park Road and as Jean lived in Andover Road, I would drop the rent in to her once a month. All the while the bungalow was empty I kept the garden tidy. As we got closer to the date when Wates would have to pay up or lose their deposit, we decided to see if we could get a bridging loan to tide us over to that date. I approached my bank and they required £3,000 just to set it up. When I told a friend, he said *"Go and see my bank manager in Romsey. Tell him I recommended you"*. For the first time over the past two years here was someone who told us exactly what would happen and what to do and if we wanted a bridging loan it would cost £300 to set it up. He said *"Wates won't pay until the last possible date. Tell Anne and Jean you will buy on that day and if this happens, as it will, you won't need the loan"*. And it happened exactly as he said.

We have always been very grateful to Anne and Jean for their extreme patience with us during those two years. I remember the kind words one of them said to me one day. *"Mum would have liked you to have her garden"*. In October 1999 we left the bungalow on the nursery where I had been born and lived all my life, except for the two years when we lived in a caravan next door. I had still been sleeping in the bedroom I was born in. I think because the last two years had been such a worry and on the nursery most of the greenhouses and buildings had been knocked down, I was only too pleased to leave. We hired a large van. David, Andrew and Jackie's Dad, David, moved us up the road to 11 Rozelle Close. On the day of the move our friends Anne and Ray arrived with lunch at about 12.30. It was our first meal in our new bungalow. We very soon settled in and took much of our time deciding what alterations we would make. Linda Brown, who had been the architect for the new hall, agreed to draw up some plans of the alterations we wanted. She also oversaw the work while it was being carried out. It was a bit traumatic living in the bungalow while the alterations were being done. Our favourite expression while it was going on was *"It will be nice when it's finished"*. I spent a lot of my life, especially latterly, talking to and helping people with their gardens, never really having a proper garden of my own, just a piece of land on the nursery. I now have a real garden of my own and can practise what I have been preaching to other people. I just wanted to create a natural garden, not too formal, a cottage garden, if there ever was such a thing. I wanted to go on growing plants, which is my real love. Somewhere I could see them come to fruition. I also have a small greenhouse where I can get in in the spring and sow my seeds and take cuttings, which can be planted out in the garden later on. Being a nurseryman growing plants to sell means you never see many of them come to fruition and flower. I can now see them from seed to flower to seed again. I also like growing my own vegetables and am amazed how much I am able to produce from a very small plot of ground. I spent my life growing plants for a living and I am still never happier than in the garden with my plants.

I do have other interests and still play bowls indoors in the winter with Anne and Ray, David and Peter. I gave up playing outside a few years ago. I have taken up swimming again and joined the Spirit Club at the Holiday Inn in Eastleigh. I try to go three times a week, usually leaving home just after 7.00 a.m. and meeting up with my friend Ken at 7.45 a. m. We swim for about three quarters of an hour, chatting as we go. It's usually the same people swimming at the same time every day, so it's quite a sociable swim and I have made quite a few new friends. Another thing we like to do since we retired is go out to lunch to different pubs and restaurants. At present our favourite is the Fox and Hounds at Crawley. I have tried to cut back my involvement with the village to a couple of clubs which I feel I can still contribute to. The Gardening Club and the History Group, where I am asked questions about gardening and the past happenings in the village. It is nice to know when you retire that some of the little bits of knowledge and experience you may have gathered over the years are of interest to others.

What is life if, full of care,
We have no time to stand and stare.

No time to stand beneath the boughs
And stare as long as sheep and cows.

No time to see, when woods we pass,
Where squirrels hide their nuts in grass.

No time to see, in broad daylight,
Streams full of stars, like skies at night.

No time to turn to Beauty's glance,
And watch her feet, how they can dance.

No time to wait till her mouth can
Enrich that smile her eyes began.

A poor life this if, full of care,
We have no time to stand and stare.

W. H. Davies

Mum and Dad celebrating their diamond wedding with a telegram from the Queen

The family celebrating together from left: John, Dad, Mum, Anne, myself and Richard in front

Tape 17
Contemplations

Looking back today over the last 80 years I realise how fortunate I have been to spend all my life in a wonderful part of the country here in central Hampshire, surrounded by rolling countryside containing so much of interest, the downs, valleys, rivers, woods and open fields which I have been able to wonder and wander over all my life. When I was working on the nursery and perhaps we had been very busy and life was getting a bit stressful, I would occasionally stroll down to our little copse in the bottom corner and look across the fields, where sometimes the Hereford cattle which belonged to the farm would be grazing. In the distance was the line of beech trees on Three Maids Hill, turning to the left, I would see the paddocks of Littleton Stud which were laid out with much foresight by Mr. Talbot of Littleton Manor in the early part of the twentieth century. He used great imagination with his choice of different varieties of trees planted between the paddocks where, as a wartime schoolboy, I had chased rabbits in the corn and helped gather in the harvest by leading the heavy horses in the harvest field. In the spring the trees between the paddocks and the beech on the hill would provide a multitude of different greens, the pale green of the beech to the darker evergreen and sometimes I would hear the cuckoo calling in the distance. As the summer went on the different coloured greens would tend to merge together and in the autumn they would turn into a multitude of colours, from yellow to orange to red to brown. When looking at the view after the great storm of 1987 I wondered what the large mounds of white were between the paddocks. After looking at them for a while I realised they were the roots of the large trees which had blown over during the storm. They were a good example of how the trees roots just grow in the soil sitting on top of the chalk. During the winter the view changed again, especially if it had snowed. Sometimes large drifts could be seen where the snow had been blown up under the hedges. The brown form of a covey of partridges could be seen showing above the snow and the larger single brown form would be that of a hare. Near me under the hedge the tracks of a rabbit were often shown and the snow could show the pattern of a pheasant's wing when it had taken off when alarmed. In the far corner of the field where the cattle grazed was a very old walnut tree where two or three times in my lifetime, usually during February, a spring would bubble up out of the ground and the water could be seen glistening in the sun, which showed up even more when the Army built their rifle range which formed a dam. The view looking over the field where the cattle grazed no longer exists. It is now a small wood planted some 20 years ago as part of the training ground for the Sir John Moore barracks.

Now I have moved up and across the village the view I have is in the opposite direction. When I'm working in the garden and my back begins to ache, as it often seems to these days, I straighten up and wander to the fence and look over the old church gate, which needed a home a few years ago, so I placed it as a focal point at the end of my garden. I look across the field where the horses are grazing; sometimes there may be a couple of foals nestling up to their mothers. At the far side of the field is Manor Lane, or Littleton Lane, but it was always known to us kids as Dolly Lane because of the telephone poles which ran along its length. They had a large number of insulators which held the telephone line. The insulators, or dollies as they were called by us, were tempting targets for naughty boys to throw stones at, or even worse a catapult. Over the lane and looking west are the woods of Northwood Park where once there was a large house which was occupied by Claysmore School. I remember Dad talking about playing cricket in the grounds. The house was occupied by British and American troops during the war, but was demolished shortly after. The woods we can see are a mixture of beech, spruce and evergreen conifers which give a striped effect with the different greens. In the centre of our view, hiding behind the large trees, is Lainston House Hotel, once the private residence of the Bostock family, who at one time owned most of the land in Littleton. To the left of the house is an avenue of lime trees and in the valley the road winding its way through them up to Sparsholt, a road we travelled many times in my younger days when visiting aunts and uncles at the bakery in Sparsholt. If we walked we would take the short cut, taking the footpath through the avenue. Once we boys were walking through when we spotted a walnut tree away from the path and started to look for any walnuts which might have fallen when the owner, Mrs. Craig-Harvey, came along and told us off and said *"The path's over there"*. Looking over the top of the avenue of trees I can see the fields which were once part of Sparsholt Downs. These border the woods which are part of Crab Wood and these provide a sea of bluebells in the spring. So I can still see the wonderful display of colours in the different seasons of the year. Unfortunately I have only heard the cuckoo calling once since we moved here ten years ago. Because we live in the highest part of the village we have the added bonus of seeing wonderful sunsets which seem to fill the whole sky with colour, making the woods look as if they are on fire as the sun sets behind them.

Having lived in the village all my life so many places or things bring back a memory of a story or happening. When I come across a certain tree I may recall when I climbed it or when I found a mistle thrush's nest in the fork of a branch. It could be the chestnut tree I fell out of when collecting conkers for medical use during the war and nearly landed up in hospital myself. When I pass a certain hedge by the road I can see the nest of a yellowhammer which could always be found there. When I pass Lower Farm wonderful memories come back of the many hours spent there in school holidays and weekends when my ambition was to be a farmer. I can still remember the thrill of being allowed by the carter, Dick Harding, to follow the team of three large carthorses pulling a two furrow plough and the smell of the soil as it was turned over. The next field was where we often found mushrooms. Another field which often jogs my memory is the one next to the steep hill in Dolly Lane. It was there we would sledge on moonlight nights. The problem was that there was a wooden rail fence at the bottom which we had to duck to go under and finish up in the lane. Unfortunately one night Eddy Gill forgot to duck and got a rather nasty shock.

Sometimes when I am going down Kennel Lane I remember the time when John, myself and a friend were freewheeling down the hill in one of John's home-made trucks. This was steered by a piece of thick string fixed to the front axle. We were swerving from one side of the road to the other when a car appeared, not a very common occurrence in those days. The friend pulled the string to avoid the car, when the string broke. Luckily he had the presence of mind to kick the front axle of the truck with his boot and we finished upside down on the bank. In the process I got a rather large gash on my knee, but at least we didn't finish up under the car.

I am fortunate to have lived near the ancient capital of Wessex, Winchester, with all its history. How being part of it also holds many memories. Apart from VE night and the crowds in the Broadway, it is the Guildhall which brings back so many happy memories with the Winchester Horticultural Society in the autumn, where long tables stretched the length of the hall with many vases of chrysanthemums of all shapes and sizes. In the spring it is the opera memories which I cherish. One memory which still comes to mind vividly is playing the lieutenant of the tower in Yeoman of the Guard standing in the wings waiting to go on while the execution scene is building up on stage. The music and drama create the tension of the situation, making the hairs tingle on the back of your neck.

I suppose it is rather unusual to have lived in the same village all one's life. So many of the young of the village had to move on because of their jobs or because they could not afford the high price of property. Until I moved up the village ten years ago to Rozelle Close I had been sleeping in the bedroom where I was born. No wonder I sometimes feel I am like the old village yokel! Littleton has always had a thriving community and I have enjoyed being part of it. I don't think I could live somewhere which didn't have a community spirit. I am often asked the question *"How is it that Littleton has so much going for it?"* I think there must be several reasons. One may be that right back to before and after the First World War, as the village developed, if the residents wanted something they had to get on and do it for themselves, unlike many villages where they had a Lord of the Manor to rule over the village and provide facilities for them. Perhaps because the inhabitants of Littleton worked for what they had, they appreciated it more. I remember my old headmaster was very fond of saying *"What you get for nothing you value at that price"*. There has always been a good mixture of folk from most walks of life, which meant a wide range of talents who were able to step in and perform the task to be done.

Life and work on the nursery changed out of all recognition during my life. As a small boy I can just remember Grandad with his market garden and his vegetable round with horse and cart. When I left school and started work during the later days of the Second World War, Dad had his nursery at Littleton where he grew his produce and the shop in Winchester where he sold it. Here he proudly advertised that everything sold in the shop was grown on the nursery at Littleton. During the Second World War, and for some years after, we spent most of our time growing vegetables and fruit, both inside the greenhouses and out. We had to be able to do everything in the business, which included a large amount of digging, to floral work, to making wreaths and wedding bouquets, and dealing with customers. As the austerity conditions of the war and after began to ease we began to grow more flowers and bedding plants. As trade increased we built much bigger greenhouses with automatic heating and watering to produce flowers on a much larger scale for wholesale. In time this changed when the garden centre idea came about, and we closed the shop in Winchester. The whole business had changed out of all recognition. I think the speed with which things had changed must have been faster in my life than at any time in previous history. I expect when my granddaughters are as old as I am now they will be saying the same. I try to avoid talking too much about the good old days, perhaps it's because Dad used to say when he was old *"Don't talk to me about the good old days; they were for some, but not for the majority"*. He had to work long hours, 6 a.m. to 6 p. m. in the summer, for a low wage. That must be one of the major differences in my lifetime, most, if not all, are better off financially than in my boyhood of the 1930s. I'm not so sure about being happier.

In those times the village was much smaller than it is now and nearly everyone knew each other and everything that was going on. Most of the members of the sports teams, clubs and church would have lived in the village. Over the years this has changed, with the population being more mobile, people joining from other villages and Winchester. Perhaps one of the reasons the clubs and church are so successful is the fact that outsiders have always been made very welcome. Transport has also played its part. Dad used to say he had seen the buses come and go in his lifetime. When I was at school we either had to walk, ride our bikes or catch the bus. There were very few who had cars and those who did found it difficult to get petrol during the war years, some were left in the garage for the duration. After the war cars gradually increased and the buses got less until they nearly vanished altogether. It is only recently they have become slightly more frequent, with the introduction of bus passes for the retired.

If you have persevered and read my story through, you will realise I haven't travelled very far, for here again for these times I must be a bit of a freak. I have never been out of the country and have never flown and as far as computers are concerned, they have left me behind. The words used are a foreign language to me. In spite of being left behind in many ways, I feel lucky to have lived where I have and to have been born and lived my life in Littleton, surrounded by my wonderful family and friends and still surrounded by much beautiful countryside. In spite of spending all my life working on the nursery, now I am retired I am never happier than working in my own garden and still living by the seasons of the year. I enjoy doing all the little jobs in their season, but the one I enjoy the most, like Dad, is at my potting shed bench potting up the plants. I don't have to mix my compost like Dad did, mine comes in bags, most likely without any soil in it at all, and there is no smell of bonemeal or fishmeal.

May the road rise up to meet you.
May the wind be always at your back.
May the sunshine warm upon your face;
the rains fall soft upon your fields and until we meet again,
may God hold you in the palm of his hand.

Traditional Gaelic Blessing

Andrew and Nicky's wedding

David and Jackie's wedding

A bedtime story with Kate and Samantha

Kate helping me on the nursery

Having a cup of tea with friends from the gardening club when I had the garden open

Hereford cattle grazing in the field at the back of the nursery. The walnut tree is centre left where the springs sometimes rise. This scene is now a wood and a rifle range

The view from my back garden

With Samantha and Kate in my spring garden sat on my eightieth birthday present

With Connie

LITTLETON from the North West

Littleton in 2001 from the North West with the old village in the foreground and the Recreation ground with the sports pitches and village hall in the centre. The road can be seen winding its way to Winchester, top right, with the Sir John Moore Barracks at the top of the picture and Harestock in the distance.
(My thanks to Mrs Sheila Trussler for her kind permission to reproduce this fine picture painted by her late husband David which now hangs in the entrance to the Littleton and Harestock Millennium Memorial Hall. **I consider it to be a very appropriate picture to end my story. AH)**

We made it! After many months of Austen producing the tapes and Pam typing them up and Connie proofreading we are now just about finished. Pam and I have been amazed at how Austen saw what he was aiming for and stuck to the task throughout. It was an incredible journey for him, sometimes painful often joyful and other than a few months during the summer when the needs of the garden or family took over he stuck to the task.

Now it is time for a last 'brushing-up' and the next stage is to get everything off to the printers for a draft copy and I know we all await the final result with great interest.

By the time you read these words you will have a copy of Austen's story in your hands and we all sincerely hope that you will have enjoyed reading it as much as we have enjoyed producing it.

Barbara Elsmore
April 2011